The *Turnabout* Programme

Dr. Carol Goldfus

Enid Korn

© Copyright 2004 Dr Carol Goldfus and Enid Korn.
All rights reserved. No part of this publication may be reproduced, stored in a retrieval system, or transmitted, in any form or by any means, electronic, mechanical, photocopying, recording, or otherwise, without the written prior permission of the authors.

Note for Librarians: a cataloguing record for this book that includes Dewey Decimal Classification and US Library of Congress numbers is available from the Library and Archives of Canada. The complete cataloguing record can be obtained from their online database at: www.collectionscanada.ca/amicus/index-e.html
ISBN 1-4120-2955-4

TRAFFORD

This book was published *on-demand* in cooperation with Trafford Publishing. On-demand publishing is a unique process and service of making a book available for retail sale to the public taking advantage of on-demand manufacturing and Internet marketing. On-demand publishing includes promotions, retail sales, manufacturing, order fulfilment, accounting and collecting royalties on behalf of the author.

Offices in Canada, USA, UK, Ireland, and Spain
book sales for North America and international:
Trafford Publishing, 6E–2333 Government St.
Victoria, BC V8T 4P4 CANADA
phone 250 383 6864 toll-free 1 888 232 4444
fax 250 383 6804 email to orders@trafford.com
book sales in Europe:
Trafford Publishing (UK) Ltd., Enterprise House, Wistaston Road Business Centre
Crewe, Cheshire CW2 7RP UNITED KINGDOM
phone 01270 251 396 local rate 0845 230 9601
facsimile 01270 254 983 orders.uk@trafford.com
order online at:
www.trafford.com/robots/04-0783.html

10 9 8 7 6

To David

Without whom this book would not have been written

Contents

Introduction

Dr Carol Goldfus – A Personal Perspective

I first became involved in treating people with dyslexia fifteen years ago, when I was asked by a friend to help her daughter who was experiencing severe problems at school. This was my first case of a child with dyslexia. Together, we learned what her problems really were and how to overcome them. Since then, my work with dyslexic people has continued intensively and I have successfully treated many hundreds of dyslexic children and adults.

During this period, I have spent much of my working life studying the theoretical basis of dyslexia and other learning disabilities and developing practical methods for helping children, teenagers and adults to overcome them. Having taught many dyslexic people on an intensive one-to-one basis, I have evolved a particular approach to combating their learning difficulties, and I have developed a programme of training exercises that has proved to be effective in real life, for a wide range of conditions. This programme is called the 'Turnabout', for that is exactly what it is. The Turnabout Programme has enabled a large number of children and adults with dyslexia or with other severe learning problems, to turn around their education and their lives. This is a co-ordinated programme of treatments that I expect to succeed.

As my success in this field has become more widely known, I have had people referred to me who have been emotionally upset and sometimes very disturbed. Many have been in despair at being unable to solve their learning problems. Indeed, a high proportion of my students had previously been through the whole range of available assistance, including specialised teaching, individual coaching, child psychiatrists and special schools. None of these measures were able to give them any real help and, only too often, each attempt and its subsequent failure, brought about greater discouragement. I am able to say that however severe their problems, and whatever their initial difficulties, everyone who has carried out my programme has been enabled to become part of the educational mainstream.

This book has been written following the many phone calls, e-mails and pleas for help from both children and their parents and also as a result of interaction within my lectures as a teacher trainer. I have decided that the time has come to spread more widely, the practical aspects of the Turnabout Programme.

My First Dyslexic Student

My first student with dyslexia was Nora, my friend's daughter. She was my introduction to an intriguing and initially baffling field; children who find the acquisition of reading and writing to be difficult and indeed, sometimes impossible. Until my friend brought Nora to meet me, I had never been involved with people with learning difficulties. I had mainly been concerned with the more academic students, who wanted to excel in their studies and to pass their final examinations with the best possible results.

Nora was quite different, and I now realise that her situation was not untypical. Nora had always been articulate, inquisitive, and outgoing and, until she started at secondary school, her parents had never even considered that there might be a problem. When they were first confronted with the true facts, they thought that a mistake had been made. They then realised that, notwithstanding her varied and intelligent conversation, their daughter could not read or write properly. Throughout her early years, it had been assumed that Nora was bright; although she was constantly being told that she could do much better, if only she could be more organized and complete her work on time. The reality of the situation was that Nora's greatest success was her ability to bluff all around her into thinking that she was coping.

Facing up to the challenge of teaching Nora, and finding the root cause of her problem, was intriguing and perplexing. At our first meeting, I was presented with an extraordinary contradiction. Here was a child who could talk on many topics, who could express herself fluently and who, on the surface, would need little or no help. But, as we first attempted to read a book, it was apparent that she had some very particular difficulties that I had not previously encountered. Nora sometimes read the letters incorrectly, she found that the lines jumped, she skipped words and letters, and she wrote many of her letters back to front; all of which became most frustrating for both of us.

It was soon very apparent that these difficulties had been there for many years, but had been concealed by her brilliant verbal skills, her bubbly personality and her ability to cover-up her real problems. Nora and I together, developed and experimented with many mental exercises, targeted to correct and to modify her condition. Much of our early work was on the basis of trial and error until we began to concentrate on those exercises that were effective.

It was through Nora I began to comprehend that constant failure could damage the personality of even the most talented of people. I became aware of the importance of self-image and self-esteem and I started to understand the role that parents can play in sustaining a child's self belief, even though there might be grave difficulties within the classroom.

Most of my work in this field has been with older children of secondary school age. Many of these young people had been seriously set back in confidence and self-esteem, following years of disappointment and frustration. From my interaction with the emotional problems of these older children, it has become apparent that the solution cannot just be restricted to addressing their mental capabilities.

Gradually, my methods evolved into a multi-facetted approach. I realised that firstly and most importantly, we must confront and put right the underlying weaknesses and conditions that have prevented people with dyslexia from being able to read and write correctly and have held them back from realising their potential. At the same time, we must rebuild and re-establish the individual's self-confidence, which the years of failure have undermined. And finally, at the end of the process, we must give teenage children some positive guidance and assistance that will enable them to become integrated into the learning environment of a secondary school and to be able to succeed there. The three aspects of the Turnabout Programme, the retraining of the mental capabilities through an extensive range of exercises, the enhancement of self-esteem and the assistance with secondary school life; each is encompassed within the body of this book.

For younger children of primary school age, the emphasis on rebuilding self-esteem is still needed, but for these children it is usually sufficient to give them the mental retraining that will enable them to read and to write. After that and within a supportive classroom environment, they are usually able to re-establish their self-confidence without very much additional support or guidance.

During the evolution of the Turnabout Programme and based upon the assessment and treatment of many people, I have come to one very fundamental conclusion. The multiplicity of symptoms that are gathered together under the heading of dyslexia, do not represent a single 'state'; instead they must be seen as a series of conditions that are holding people back and preventing them from making progress. The exercises for the brain that are used within the Turnabout programme, are constructed to counteract this 'holding-back' phenomenon and thereby allow people to progress at a rate which is appropriate for them as individuals. There are many who consider dyslexia to be untreatable. I now know this not to be true.

In contrast to the widely accepted approach, I look upon people who have been labelled as dyslexic, as part of the normal range of learners. I have no sympathy with the view that the learning problems associated with dyslexia are, in some way, the 'flipside' of genius. There are indeed some very prominent people with dyslexia, but for every person who succeeds in spite of this condition, there are many tens of thousands whose lifetime prospects are very greatly diminished by it.

We should not be misled by the fact that some dyslexic people manage to attain higher education, both through their great personal determination, and the assistance and understanding of universities that accept their written work with its dyslexic characteristics. These students may be helped and accommodated by being allowed to take examinations verbally or by being given additional time; but these are palliative measures and they do not address the root causes of dyslexia. By contrast, there are very many more individuals who leave school knowing very little and with potential employment and social problems. Many of these people with dyslexia have great unrealised potential; there is no reason why they should not succeed in life. Everyone must be given the opportunity to overcome his or her difficulties and to succeed. The motto of the Turnabout Programme is "From Failure to Excellence" and this is the ultimate aim of this book.

In recent years, there has been a startling increase in the number of children who have been labelled as having 'attention deficit disorder' and the more extreme version, with what is described as 'hyperactivity'. I have found that many of the exercises that we have developed to treat dyslexia are also applicable and equally effective for people with an attention deficit disorder. Many people with attention deficit problems have undertaken the Turnabout Programme, and with successful results.

The Turnabout Programme is set out in this book as a 'package' of exercises, all of which can be carried out by parents with their own children or by friends or family of dyslexic adults. The Turnabout Programme needs only a minimal investment in equipment, but does involve a significant commitment of time. I know very well, from the many children that I have helped, that there is no magic wand that can be waved to change things overnight. It can be a tough path to follow, as children with learning difficulties are often not easy to handle or to persuade. But it is a task that needs to be undertaken, as it may be the only chance you have of halting your child's inevitable slide towards failure and instead, making a turnabout towards success.

As much of my own work has been done with secondary school children and with adults, I have been pleased to co-operate on this book with my co-author and friend, Enid Korn, who has a lifetime of experience within the primary sector of education. Enid's knowledge of children's problems has assisted in adapting the Turnabout Programme, so that it is readily applicable to younger children. Indeed, the younger the child can be trained the better; the sooner problems are identified, the more easily they can be resolved.

To encourage you, the parents, that you can indeed make a difference, we have included within this book, stories of some of the most severely affected people who we have helped; children and adults who have come to the Turnabout programme in despair and who we have enabled to go back into the world and to succeed. The path is not always straightforward, but the effort is always worthwhile.

Returning to Nora, my very first dyslexic student. Nora did indeed make a remarkable turnabout. She gradually learned to read and write properly and, in the end, she was successful at her secondary school. Nora went on to an outstanding academic career at a major university and she is now fulfilling the great potential that her parents always believed that she possessed. She is employed as a translator of popular novels and also appears on radio and television shows, discussing books and films. Although Nora has achieved considerable success in her profession, she still remembers her difficult years and often reminds others that life is not always easy, and that sometimes you have to work very hard to overcome the obstacles that you encounter.

There are many tens of thousands of other children who are in need of help and I know, only too well, the stresses and strains that such children can impose on parents and indeed on the whole family. Throughout the years, I have been struck, again and again, by the contrast between the initial despair of the parents and children in these situations and then later, by the joy and the sparkle in everyone's eyes when the turnabout occurs. The gratitude and emotion of the parents never fails to bring tears to my own eyes.

I welcome the opportunity of helping many more people, by sharing the success of this programme. I very much hope that you experience the same lift in your lives as those people that I have worked with directly. I particularly look forward to hearing about your successes and that you join the family of people who have been helped by the Turnabout Programme.

Dr Carol Goldfus

Section 1

Introducing The Turnabout Programme

Chapter One

Introducing the Turnabout Programme

This is the one chapter that I have written as myself, Enid Korn, and not jointly with Dr Carol Goldfus. In this chapter, I will tell you a little about ourselves, the authors, who we are and why we decided to write this book. I will give an overview of the contents and explain how you should go about using this book to help your own child. Most importantly, I will answer the question, "Why did we decide to launch an educational book primarily for you, the parents and not for the teachers?"

Carol Goldfus and I are both educationalists. Carol is head of department in a large teacher training college and is also involved with university research in her specialist field. She has worked with severely affected dyslexic children and adults for over fifteen years and more recently, she has been involved with children with attention deficit problems. During all of this time, she has achieved unparalleled success.

I am an independent educational consultant working in the U.K. I have taught in the English primary school system for over twenty years. I am also an Ofsted accredited inspector of primary schools and have visited many schools in this capacity since 1994. Both Carol Goldfus and I have four children of our own.

I am very pleased and excited to have had the opportunity to contribute to this unique book, based on the work of Dr. Carol Goldfus, who is an outstanding educationalist and innovator. She has achieved extraordinary results, with both children and adults diagnosed as dyslexic, many of whom had previously been given little effective help by teachers or psychologists. She has changed the future prospects for these people; she has enabled them to go back into the mainstream of education and she has changed their lives.

Some of those that Dr. Goldfus has helped have been transformed from being educational failures, to achieving success at university and obtaining professional qualifications. But not all people are academic. Some of her students have been made very happy just by being given the skills for life; being able to take telephone messages, read newspapers and magazines, look up train timetables; all the many small things that most of us take for granted. Not least, these people now have a much wider range of jobs open to them. The heart-warming and encouraging stories of some of the people who have participated in the Turnabout Programme, feature extensively in this book.

Many people in education have accepted that dyslexia is a condition apart and that it is largely impossible to remedy. The Times Educational Supplement, in an article in February 2003, stated that "there is no cure" and that "children respond best with information in a non written form". Dr Goldfus has shown us that this whole body of assumptions is based on a failure to comprehend the fundamental nature of the problem. Once we understand and accept that dyslexic people are like the rest of us, but are on an extreme end of a learning continuum, then our whole approach should change. We need, as Dr Goldfus has done with such success, to look at the blockages in the path of learning that have caused the problem and we must set out to remove these obstacles or to bypass them. If we do this, then the normal educational processes in our schools can begin to be effective for these children.

Dr Goldfus has achieved great success in a most complex and difficult field, working with teenagers and adults with dyslexia. Many of the people she has helped were in a state of despair, following years of frustration and of failure. To complement her work with adults and older children, I have been able to adapt the programme so that it can be equally effective for the younger school age child. When dyslexic conditions become established, they are rarely resolved by conventional teaching. If young children have problems which undermine their learning, then the sooner we can work with them in the right way, the quicker the problems will be resolved and the children will be spared many years of ineffective schooling and upsetting experiences.

The Turnabout Programme is the product of fifteen years of continuous development, establishing what works in practice, for real people with serious problems. But, perhaps the most exciting aspect, is that it is also being verified by the latest and most up-to-date theories and research into cognition. (i.e. how the brain actually works).

A Book For The Parents

Why have we chosen to introduce the Turnabout Programme through the parents and not through the school system? There are some very sound educational and psychological reasons for adopting this approach and these are set out in the following paragraphs.

Partnership

The Turnabout programme contains some deceptively simple mental exercises, which address the underlying causes of dyslexia and other learning difficulties. The effect of the exercises is to help a child's brain to find a route around the blockages that have prevented him or her from learning in the school setting. These exercises are very clearly set out and do not require specialist skills to administer. Parents can do them as readily as trained teachers. As the exercises take effect, they enable the day-to-day activities of the school to begin and continue to be successful, in a way that they were not previously. The Turnabout exercises in no way compete with the school. On the contrary, they complement the work of the school.

In today's world of education, our schools see themselves in partnership with the parents. By the parents taking the lead in carrying out the Turnabout exercises with their own children, this partnership can be strengthened and consolidated.

The Turnabout training will succeed in improving your child's capabilities and this will subsequently be reflected back into school and will show up in better reading, writing and mathematics. Your child's school may see this improvement as directly resulting from their own efforts and this is OK. You are not competing for recognition or glory; both you and the school only want what is best for your child.

One To One Attention

For the Turnabout exercises to be most effective, they need to be carried out on a one to one basis, with you and your child working together without distraction or interference. Although the education system in England is giving increasingly greater attention to children with 'special educational needs', it may not be practical for this one to one relationship to be applied for sufficient time, at your own child's school. Whatever the outside pressures, parents can usually make sure that they make the time available to help their child in such a crucial matter.

Helping The Demoralized Child

It is also important to consider the attitude of children who have had learning problems. These children are almost invariably demoralised or de-motivated by their inability to do all the very basic things that their friends find so easy. This applies to children of all ages. I have seen children as young as five years of age, reluctant to try some very straightforward activities, because they have already begun to fail in other areas and do not want to do so again. By contrast, another child in the same group who has never experienced failure, will be uninhibited, will try different approaches and will learn and develop through these experiences. This small gap at the beginning of school life can become a chasm by the time children are of secondary school age.

By carrying out these exercises at home, we will be giving children of all ages some relief from the pressure and tension that can build up within the classroom setting. The work is done in private, away from the scrutiny of their peers. The training and the gradual improvement will not be under the spotlight and will be all the better for that.

Attention Deficit Problems

In recent years, there has been an alarming rise in the number of children with attention deficit disorder. I rarely visit a school today that does not have some children with attention deficit problems, often with hyperactivity. This was not the case ten years ago when I started as an inspector. While the great increase in the number of children identified as having 'special needs' is a reflection of the caring approach in education, there are still many problems remaining to be solved.

Until now, attention deficit disorder has been seen as a condition to be contained rather than resolved, exactly as with dyslexia. And again, as for dyslexia, the basis of the Turnabout Programme is to treat the underlying causes, aiming to correct the condition and not just to ameliorate it. Many of the remedial exercises that we describe within the book are effective for both dyslexia and for attention deficit problems, and indeed, many children are burdened by both conditions. The rationale for the Turnabout approach to attention deficit problems is described more fully in chapter three.

The Turnabout Exercises

The Turnabout Programme consists of a number of straightforward and comprehensive mental exercises that redress the underlying causes of dyslexia and attention deficit problems. It is not a literacy programme in itself, but it underpins the work of the schools by strengthening the processes within the brain that facilitate proper reading and writing

Within the book we have set out guidance for parents, helping you to put together your own programme, to address the particular needs of your child. There are some core exercises, which are a vital and essential part of the programme and there are other exercises, which, whilst they are also beneficial, are not essential and can be selected for use when appropriate. You should carry out the core exercises and whichever of the occasional exercises seem right for your child. Do not worry too much whether or not to put in any particular exercise outside of the core set. All children are different and all have different conditions and requirements. All of the exercises may have some benefit for your child.

Ideally, you will need to take some twenty to thirty five minutes for each training session, three or four times a week. The most important thing is continuity. You should find a specific time of day to sit down with your child, undisturbed and once you have set a time, do your best to keep to it. At a maximum level of around two hours per week, the programme does not impose greatly in time, although we recognise the difficulty for busy parents with large families or outside commitments, to find the time just to concentrate on helping one particular child. But this one to one interaction is necessary; with minimal distraction by mobile phones, other children in the family, or any thing else, if you want to give your child the opportunity to realise his or her full potential.

The exercises are explained in a very clear way and members of the family other than parents, can also help to administer them for the child. We do not underestimate the role of grandparents and the help that they can give within this retraining process. If your children are fortunate enough to have a grandparent living nearby, then the administration of the programme can be shared and many older people are only too pleased to spend some time with their grandchildren and to help them with their problems.

We believe that it is most important that parents and others who are helping children overcome their learning difficulties, should understand the purpose of each individual exercise. To that end, we have explained, in a clear and non-technical manner, the underlying theory and principles behind the Turnabout Programme. Section two of the book describes the way that spoken and written information is perceived and remembered, and the particular deficiencies in these processes that can bring about the conditions that we are attempting to remedy. We have done this so that when you carry out each exercise with your child, you will know why it is included and the particular weakness that it is there to address.

The time that will elapse before the improvement in mental capabilities is reflected in better reading and writing, will vary widely between one person and another and will depend on the age of the individual and the seriousness of the condition at the start. You may not see any changes in your child's capabilities for three months. For some seriously affected people, it has taken the best part of a year before there has been a major breakthrough. But this timescale must be viewed against the fact that some young people, when they started the Turnabout Programme, had been in education for ten years or more, with scarcely any progress at all.

Within chapter sixteen we have set out some practical guidance for parents, on how to go about organising and managing the training of their own child. Although the individual exercises are straightforward to administer, a sustained programme of training a child will be a new experience for many people.

Teenagers With Problems

Many of the greatest successes of the Turnabout programme have been with severely dyslexic teenage children, some of whom started the programme with social and emotional difficulties, alongside their educational problems. Dr Goldfus has recognised the vital importance that must be attached to improving the self-confidence and self-esteem of these young people, in parallel with the improvement in their educational capabilities. She has established a working methodology for teenage children that addresses their self-esteem issues and treats these matters as seriously as the learning problems.

The emotional problems of the typical teenager are sometimes magnified by a history of educational failure, compared to family and friends. In chapter eighteen, we give some guidance on helping young people to come to terms with previous lack of success. We encourage them to attempt to put past failures behind them, accept that we all fail at some point in our lives and understand that today's setbacks can very quickly be left behind. Although the guidance is directed mainly at the parents of teenage children, much of the advice and the principles can also apply to encouraging younger children. Children of primary age can very quickly lose confidence, particularly in competitive and successful schools, when they do not themselves match this success. But on the other hand, young children can very quickly regain their self-belief, as soon as they begin to recognise some achievement of their own.

Returning to Academic Life

The final chapter of the book provides guidance on a return to active learning. It may be seen as overly optimistic by the parents of a child with severe problems, but we believe that it will be needed. When teenage children, as a result of the Turnabout programme, become capable (perhaps for the first time), of being part of the learning process at secondary school, they may still not understand how to go about it. They may not have acquired even the very basic study skills, such as understanding what you need to know (and what you don't need to know), and being able to arrange and marshal facts. Those of us who have never had major learning problems, will probably have assimilated these study skills gradually and progressively, but the young person whose capabilities suddenly start to blossom, may need to learn them more quickly and urgently. Chapter nineteen of the book gives some excellent guidance for these particular children (and indeed for other students), to help them cope with and manage the learning of many subjects within the secondary school environment. Within this chapter, we set out a ten-point plan for handling the world of school, university or indeed, for coping within any other training programme. This is a comprehensive framework for any new or existing learner. These skills are rarely taught at school and for some families, this chapter alone will be worth the time spent reading the book.

A Wonderful Opportunity

I am totally convinced of the validity of the Turnabout programme and of its widespread applicability. The potential benefit to hundreds of thousands of children and adults, throughout the U.K. and worldwide, is immeasurable.

Most people working within education are in a results-orientated environment. Teachers' performance is measured by their pupils' success in tests and examinations; school inspectors are encouraged to judge by the evidence and by the results. The evidence for the success of the Turnabout Programme is overwhelming. Dr Goldfus has a cabinet full of letters of thanks from grateful pupils and parents. Of equal importance is the fact that no one has been through the programme, without having been 'turned about' and enabled to function properly in the classroom and in life.

I recognise that sometimes it is not easy to accept the fact that your own child has educational problems. I have also seen the difficulties that families can face when there is a child with attention deficit disorder or dyslexia. It can lead to frustration for both the child and the parents and can cause distress and upset within the family at unpredictable times. I am confident that this book and the exercises that are contained within it, will help your child to overcome these problems and will lead to enhanced family harmony.

I know that some parents of children with dyslexia have sought help for many years and from many sources, and they have been unable to find the support that they need. With this book, parents now have a way forward that gives hope for themselves and for their children. As parents, it is in your own hands. Carry out these exercises with persistence and with patience. The Turnabout programme does not purport to give an overnight solution but it is practical and it is valid, and as illustrated by the real life examples in this book, it has helped many people with very serious problems. We believe that this programme will enable you to make a turnabout in both the educational capabilities and the life prospects of your child.

Chapter Two

The Turnabout Programme and Dyslexia

During the last decade, the Turnabout Programme has successfully helped very many dyslexic children and adults. It has enabled them to read and write, after many years of unsuccessful schooling. At a time when the emphasis amongst academics and educationalists has largely been on understanding and identifying dyslexia, the Turnabout Programme has focussed on intervention and practical help. It is important that a parent of a dyslexic child, or a friend or relative of a dyslexic adult, should understand why this programme has been so effective.

What is Dyslexia?

Dyslexia is not easy to define, mainly because the term encompasses a wide and differing range of characteristics. The British Dyslexic Society describes dyslexia in very general terms as ".. a combination of abilities and difficulties defined by its characteristics that affect the learning process in one or more areas of reading, spelling, and writing". The symptoms that are described are representative of the problems that affect dyslexic people to a greater or lesser degree. They are a signal that the person has a need for help. Some of the characteristics that we describe were present in each of the participants in the Turnabout Programme, at the time that they started.

Reading

There are very specific reading problems that are typical of dyslexic people. These include:

- Confusion of letters of similar shapes, such as 'd' and 'b'
- Confusion with the sequence of letters in a word. A dyslexic child will often read 'saw' instead of 'was', or vice-versa.
- The dyslexic person is apt to lose the place in a page when attempting to read.
- Dyslexic people often cannot remember how to read very common words and therefore they need to attempt to read them phonetically (according to the sounds of the letters) every time they pick up a book.
- Some dyslexic people cannot work out words phonetically or if they can, it is only with great difficulty.
- When dyslexic children are given reading practice they can become tired very quickly; they read slowly and are thus prone to forget the beginning of a sentence by the time they reach the end.

Spelling

There are ranges of difficulties with spelling that affect dyslexic people.

- They do not properly distinguish and record in the brain the difference between similar sounding words, such as 'pin' and 'pen'.
- The English language cannot, of course, be read only phonetically and the reader needs to remember a large number of words for which the spelling is not apparently logical. A dyslexic person will frequently attempt the spelling of such words in a totally phonetic style and, for example, might spell 'says' as 'sez', or 'was' as 'woz'.
- A dyslexic person will sometimes transpose the order of the letters such as 'nda' for 'and'.
- Some people cannot absorb the rules of English spelling, such as the effect of an e at the end of a word, or 'i before e except after c'.

- Often, dyslexic children cannot remember familiar spelling patterns such as 'ight', which they will try to spell phonetically, and therefore inaccurately.

Most young children without dyslexia will exhibit initial difficulties with many of these spelling patterns, and indeed with the writing symptoms set out below. In time, they will overcome them. The dyslexic child does not respond to traditional teaching and does not learn how to apply these spelling rules.

Writing

The writing problems shown by dyslexic children are often associated with a lack of physical co-ordination. For example:

- The dyslexic child may have problems holding a pencil correctly.
- There is sometimes no consistency of size, between letters in a sentence.
- Capital letters and lower case letters are sometimes intermingled.
- Poor hand-eye coordination can make intelligible writing and accurate drawing, very difficult to achieve.

Dyslexia and the Educational System

As a direct result of their problems, dyslexic children routinely suffer great frustration at school and within their social environment. In particular, teenagers with dyslexia often have poor self-esteem and are rarely the happy and confident people they could be. Notwithstanding their educational problems, such children may well be very intelligent.

In general, the educational system in England and elsewhere, has not believed that the problems of dyslexia can be resolved. Within the primary phase of education, which in England is up to the age of eleven, children with dyslexia will be identified as having 'special educational needs'. They will usually be provided with considerable additional practice in the skills of phonics, but this only addresses the symptoms and not the causes.

At secondary schools and universities, the emphasis is usually to give assistance and concessions to dyslexic students; this often enables them to complete their studies, notwithstanding their inability to handle projects or examinations in the conventional way. Such help includes allowing additional time for examinations, allowing essays to be presented verbally or written down by someone else, an acceptance of erratic spelling and uncoordinated grammar without any loss of marks, and other similar assistance to enable dyslexic people to participate, as much as possible, in the academic world. The underlying principle that has been adopted, has been to accept the situation and to help dyslexic people come to terms with their problems and manage as best they can. However helpful and well meaning this approach is, it contains no attempt to combat or to resolve dyslexia. In the end, even if dyslexic students achieve a university degree level qualification, they may still leave the educational system unable to read and write properly. Of course, not all dyslexic people are able to undertake higher learning. Many people with dyslexia have completed their schooling, totally unable to read or write and with very little to show for twelve years within the classroom.

The Turnabout Programme

Why then has the Turnabout programme been so successful and what is it that makes it work?

The treatment of dyslexia within the Turnabout Programme differs quite fundamentally from the standard approach of the educational system. First and foremost, we do not believe that the condition is untreatable or that these apparently intractable problems cannot be resolved. Indeed, we know the very opposite to be true. Nor, within the programme, do we encourage the use of the type of concessions that are made in school or college to accommodate dyslexic people. We aim for dyslexic people to see themselves as part of the mainstream of education.

Turnabout training is particularly distinctive in that it is a 'non linguistic' process; it is not formulated on language and is unlike the learning process at school, in which the emphasis of attempting to help dyslexic children is generally based on the spoken and written word.

The foundation of the Turnabout Programme is a series of mental exercises to be carried out by dyslexic individuals, with the guidance and supervision of family, friends or teachers. These exercises have been constructed to address the underlying causes of dyslexia and not the symptoms. The exercises will develop new mental strengths and create new pathways in the brain, both of which are necessary for overcoming the difficulties of learning.

The Turnabout Programme places great emphasis on 'listening skills', the ability to properly focus on the more important information that is being heard and to disregard the rest. This is a problem for many dyslexic people and very often, a breakthrough in this matter is the gateway to improvement in many other areas. This particular topic is explained in more detail in chapter five.

There is a wide range of exercises, each of which address one or more of the main causes of dyslexia, together encompassing a number of alternative approaches. One particular exercise, or more likely a combination of many of them, will be needed and appropriate for each individual. The exercises in the book have been developed and refined through working intensively with many dyslexic children and adults. They have worked for young children, for teenagers and for adults. There is no age limit. It is never too late. On the other hand, the earlier in life the problems are addressed, the quicker and easier it will be to put things right.

Improving The Memory

One of the main reasons why the Turnabout Programme works well in practice is the emphasis that is placed on the development and the improvement of the memory. Many of these symptoms of dyslexia set out in this chapter, have weaknesses of memory as an underlying cause. The exercises provided within the programme will strengthen the memory processes of the participants.

To some people, the process of training the memory can appear both complex and formidable. It is therefore important to understand what the Turnabout training does and also what it does not do. Turnabout memory training sets out to permanently strengthen the weak memory by a number of simple and proven exercises. The parent or trainer should not feel intimidated in any way by these exercises; they are not difficult to apply nor are they too complicated for the dyslexic person to understand and accept. The exercises can sometimes seem awkward at first, but with continuous practice, the capacity of the individual to memorise spoken and written information, both instinctively and consciously, is substantially improved. Through these improvements, a major barrier that prevents some dyslexic people from being able to read at all can be progressively overcome. The Turnabout training is not just a means of providing tricks that enable those of us with a typical memory to better recall people's names or reproduce facts for examinations. It is much more than that. We are looking to make lasting changes in the complete memory process. The Turnabout Programme has helped many children and adults whose learning difficulties have been brought about, at least partially, by what is often termed a 'poor' memory.

Within the book, we have included a selection of very different stories of people who have been helped by the Turnabout Programme. Apart from the names that have been changed, all of these stories are true and accurate, and they illustrate the many different types of people who have been through the programme. These stories show the outcome of the training and the quite remarkable impact that the turnabout in their capabilities has made on their lives. At the end of this chapter is the story of Daniel, once very severely dyslexic, who at the time of writing, is near to achieving his doctorate. Chapter five contains the story of Yvonne, who became a lawyer. The stories of these students illustrate the fact that many intelligent dyslexic people have changed from failure to academic success, after participating in the Turnabout Programme.

We do not presume that all dyslexic people have the capability or the interest to pursue academic aims. Nor do we believe, as is sometimes stated, that dyslexic people are somehow different from the rest of us, with some unique complementary capabilities. People with dyslexia are a typical mix of the clever, the average and those who are not academically orientated. Within chapter fourteen, we tell the story of James who came to the Turnabout Programme with almost every one of the symptoms of dyslexia listed at the beginning of this chapter. The fact that he was able to read and write when he left school represents extraordinary progress in itself, and for James this is an achievement as great as any higher academic qualification.

The differences between the Turnabout methods and conventional classroom teaching can be illustrated by use of a sporting analogy. If we consider the game of tennis; a person who is incapable of playing a proper game because of a physical weakness or lack of agility will be unhappy and ineffective on the tennis court and repetitive practice will not make a great deal of difference. A much better alternative would be a few months in the gymnasium, working to strengthen arms, wrists and shoulders, building agility and stamina and aiming to redress the underlying weaknesses that have prevented the game being played properly. The aspiring player can then go back onto the court, find that the ball is being hit back across the net with much less effort, and is then in the position of being able to learn and to develop as a competent player.

We can look on literacy skills in the same way as physical skills. Rather than persisting with ineffective reading 'practices', if we strengthen the way the brain processes words and images, we can redress the underlying weaknesses that have prevented a person from being able to read effectively. When people, who have been fortified in this way, go back to attempting to read and write, they find that they are able to progress at a much faster rate than before.

If a child cannot remember simple common words after attempting to read them very many times, what is needed is not more intensive reading practice which can be demoralising, but training to improve the visual memory processes. After this, and with the memory working much more effectively, a child will remember common words and reading can go forward. This very simple example is sufficient to illustrate why the Turnabout Programme can be effective in helping dyslexic people, when years of schooling have not.

Why The Success?

Set out below is a summary of the points made in this chapter and some of reasons why the Turnabout Programme has been successful in treating people with dyslexia.

- Turnabout training is based on exercises which develop and strengthen the workings of the brain and which address the underlying weaknesses that have brought about the symptoms of dyslexia. This approach is very different from the conventional way of dealing with dyslexia within the educational system.
- The exercises in the programme are non-linguistic and they utilise a wide range of media such as music, dice and pictures. Appropriate exercises can be selected based on individual needs, to provide a personalised solution for each individual.
- Great emphasis is placed on improving the memory processes of the dyslexic person. Very focussed exercises strengthen both the visual memory (the ability to remember the detail of what is seen) and also the auditory memory (the ability to remember the spoken

word). Memory weaknesses are apparent in most dyslexic people; they are a major cause of their problems and they can and should be addressed. Aspects of memory are discussed in more detail in chapters six and eight.

- Many dyslexic people have an 'auditory' problem; they do not react properly to and remember what they have heard. Other dyslexic people have a 'visual' problem; they cannot visualise properly and then retain in their memory, what they have seen. Many have both auditory and visual problems. The Turnabout Programme provides corrective training for dyslexic people, whatever the combination of weaknesses that has brought about their own distinctive condition.
- Some people have only a small number of the symptoms of dyslexia, and these symptoms co-exist with strengths in other areas. For instance, some children can understand and recall what they have been told with great accuracy but have difficulty in remembering what they see. The Turnabout Programme allows the weaker areas to be targeted, by selecting those exercises that are most appropriate for each individual.
- Some dyslexic people are much more seriously affected. The Turnabout Programme has the capacity to treat even the more severe cases of dyslexia. Such people may have to work very hard within the programme and they may need to make use of the full range of the exercises. But as a parent of a severely affected dyslexic child, you can undertake the programme with the assurance that many similarly impacted people have already been helped and many more will be helped in the future
- We recognise the fact that dyslexic teenagers have often become demoralised and de-motivated by repeated disappointments at school. For these young people, improvements in their learning capabilities are inextricably linked with enhancement to their self-esteem. Chapter eighteen of this book gives guidance to parents on helping their teenage children to develop confidence and to go forward as people, in line with the improvements in their learning capabilities brought about by the Turnabout exercises.

As a parent of a child with dyslexia, you can commence these exercises with the assurance and encouragement that other children with most severe problems have made major advances through the Turnabout training. We confidently expect that you will be able to lead and assist your own child in making this most crucial turnabout.

The Story of Daniel: From Night Club Bouncer To University Lecturer

At the age of 22, Daniel was working as a bouncer in a nightclub. When he phoned Dr Goldfus for an appointment, he admitted that he was only making the call as a favour to his father. Daniel explained that he had severe dyslexia as well as attention deficit problems and said that "having seen so many people in the past, all of whom were all a waste of time, he didn't think that there was any way that he could be helped."

The answer was not what Daniel expected. He was told that the choice was his! He had to be mature enough to realise that in order to be helped he had to accept that he needed help and that he must want to be helped. On Daniel's first visit it was explained to him that, as a dyslexic, he has blockages in his ability to learn and that these can be likened to obstructions on a road - when the road directly ahead is blocked, we must seek to find another route. Training the brain to make other paths and to circumvent the blockages is what differentiates the Turnabout Programme from the other people he had seen and the other treatments he had received.

After a month's trial, Daniel resolved to continue with the programme and see what happened. It was very quickly determined that his auditory perception, often a weakness in dyslexic people, was at an unusually high level and that he was over-reacting to the very many different sound sensations around him, which was making him edgy and nervous. Working with the auditory exercises in the Turnabout Programme, brought about the resolution of his problem. As a very direct result, Daniel's sensitivity to extraneous noises was progressively reduced. As this characteristic diminished, so did his attention deficit problems.

Daniel was a body builder and well accustomed to working at exercises with great seriousness. He carried this approach through to his Turnabout training. At first, as his dyslexic problems gradually lessened, Daniel thought that he might train to become a sports instructor and his willingness to attempt anything more intellectually demanding was, unsurprisingly, constrained by his previous difficulties in school. But it was becoming obvious to all, including Daniel himself, that he was really a very intelligent man and it was his previous failures that had made him insecure. Daniel was encouraged to apply to university and he was given psychometric tests as a substitute for his lack of academic qualifications. Daniel did well in the tests and enrolled on a philosophy course.

Daniel immediately felt comfortable at the university but he needed a little extra help in the first year. Although he had progressed sufficiently to be able to read and to study, his writing was still slow Initially he was given a concession to be able to dictate some of his examination essays, for someone else to type in. By the time he reached first-degree level, some of Daniel's work was of such an exceptional standard that, together with his professor, Daniel published a joint paper on one of his specialised topics.

Daniel has continued to thrive in the demanding university environment. His written work, using the computer, has gradually become quicker and he no longer needs any assistance. He is now a lecturer at the university and he is working hard towards his doctorate. The turnabout, from bouncer to academic, has been a reward for his father whose faith in his son started the Turnabout process and it is a constant source of astonishment for Daniel himself.

Chapter Three

Understanding Attention Deficit Disorder

In today's highly technological world, our capacity to pay attention to matters of importance and priority is under more pressure than at any time in the past. Throughout the day, we can be bombarded by an extensive range of distracting stimuli, through background television, illuminated advertisements, intrusive music in many shops and many other sources. For much of the time, we are able to absorb the multiplicity of sounds and intrusive sights around us and function adequately. Nevertheless, our capacity to focus on the essential and the important can begin to be eroded and the cumulative impact of this combination of sensations can sometimes bring about an information 'overload'.

The fundamental difference for children and adults diagnosed with attention deficit is the time that it takes for them to reached this state of overload. Their capacity to absorb and to make use of the many sensations around them is very quickly overwhelmed. All of us can reach the point when the sensations that surround us become too much and we cannot focus properly on a particular task. For people with an attention deficit problem, *that state is reached very quickly.*

All people have their own individual level of tolerance to noise and to other stimuli. If measured, this could be represented as a continuum, or as a scale from low to high tolerance. People with attention deficit are at the lowest end of this scale, with little ability to tolerate sensations but we must always remember that they are on a normal scale. The reality of the situation is quite different to the general perception. Rather than a *deficit* of attention, such people suffer from absorbing and processing *too many* concurrent sensations and what we must seek to address is a situation not of deficit but of *information overload.*

Attention Deficit in Children

The range of symptoms diagnosed as Attention Deficit Disorder (ADD) has become increasingly prevalent in our schools in recent years. Children with attention deficit problems display some or all of the following characteristics.

- Are unable to concentrate on school work
- Have difficulty in sustaining attention
- Are easily distracted
- Avoid tasks that require sustained effort
- Do not seem to be listening when spoken to
- Are absent-minded and forgetful in daily activities
- Are unable to do their schoolwork, without one to one supervision
- Can become withdrawn

The more volatile children are usually diagnosed as having ADHD, the variant that encompasses 'hyperactivity' and often have such characteristics as:

- Unable to keep still during class
- Leave their seat at the wrong time
- Run and move about when it is inappropriate
- Talk excessively
- Interrupt other children in the class
- Cannot wait their turn
- Are impulsive, blurting out answers and not considering alternatives
- Other behaviour that is generally unacceptable in the classroom or at home

Children suffering from an attention deficit, usually have other educational and social problems. Even in primary school, these children can be two to four years behind their age group and very often they suffer from other serious learning difficulties. Such children can be irritable, aggressive and domineering and they may find it difficult to make and to keep friends. This inability to mix well socially will usually contribute towards unhappiness and diminished self-esteem.

During the twelve years or so that we spend within the school system, most of us will, at some time, have exhibited some of the attention deficit characteristics that have been described. But the child with an attention deficit problem exhibits many of them, most of the time and through this, proper functioning in school is disrupted.

What Attention Deficit Really Is

In order to better understand attention deficit, it can be helpful to consider the whole process of 'paying attention'. We learn in school and elsewhere through a process that is based upon the *selection* of some information, out of the totality of what is being provided. This can sometimes be done consciously and deliberately or it can be an automatic process. The process of selection of information can be broken down into three stages.

Steps in Paying Attention

1. Firstly, information is *perceived*, either by seeing words in print or on a blackboard, or hearing the spoken word or by both sights and sounds on a screen or in many other ways.
2. Secondly, information is *selected,* the important, the relevant, the significant and the interesting, is isolated from the mass of other detail.
3. And then thirdly, the selected information is *attended to*. When we have acquired our information through the first two steps of this sequence, we are able to begin to make sense of it and to establish links with other knowledge that we possess. We incorporate this new information into our total framework of present knowledge and understanding.

From birth onwards, our brain gradually becomes accustomed to this procedure of *perceiving, selecting* and then *utilising* information in this way.

The essence of the attention deficit problem arises when people come under stress, through being overloaded with a variety of sensations. This situation causes the 'thinking system' to start to close down, which acts as a protection mechanism against an overload. After some repetition, this shutting down reflex develops into an automatic response. In an educational context, this reaction will prevent proper and effective learning taking place.

We see this happening in the classroom. The child who has an attention deficit, cannot cope with the noise, the schoolmates, the worry about homework, the scope of the information being given out by the teacher and all other items of intrusive detail. The speed in which the information is being passed across by the teacher, the cumulative volume of this and of all of the surrounding sensations, causes an overload and, as a consequence, the brain shuts down. When this happens, there can be no process of perception, selection, and attention. This overload situation is the essence of attention deficit.

This scenario can cause children to immediately react and to display the symptoms known as hyperactivity. Boys will sometimes shout and become belligerent; girls may cry and run out of the room. An alternative response can be an outward show of boredom or resentment or a blank look, which is most usually a lack of engagement, precipitated by the action of the protection mechanism within the brain. The unresponsive attitude of such a child is sometimes interpreted as disobedience, or lack of interest, or a lack of commitment, and previous generations have seen the clichéd phrases of “must pay more attention”, and similar, on children’s school reports.

There are many comparable examples in everyday life. For older people, loud and intrusive music in a shop, may make the attempt to choose from a wide selection extremely uncomfortable, and when they walk out, they feel a sense of relief. In this situation, the inbuilt control system has worked and they have protected themselves from an overload of sensations.

If your own child is unable to function properly within a classroom setting and has been diagnosed as having an attention deficit problem, then the true situation is likely to be, that he or she has an inability to cope with a multiplicity of sensations and distractions. As with many things, once we properly understand the cause, then we can set about applying the remedies. Within this book, we describe a number of mental exercises that will assist you to treat the attention deficit problem in your own child. The target is to improve the capability of children to ‘discriminate’; to enable them to focus on the essential and the immediate needs, whilst still being aware of the background and less important sensations that surround them. Children who cannot give full attention to their lessons, may as a consequence, develop other educational problems. Therefore, many of the Turnabout exercises that assist children with other learning difficulties may also be applicable to children with attention deficit problems.

Development With Age

Sometimes, when children reach their teens, the characteristics of attention deficit become less prominent. Alternatively, the problems can be exacerbated by hormonal disturbances. Where the characteristics persist into adolescence, they can present a much more extreme problem, co-existing as they do with increased self-awareness and with more intense peer pressure. Teenagers with attention deficit problems are often extremely unhappy, very erratic academically and they can experience or sometimes be the cause of, serious social problems.

Attention deficit difficulties may persist into adulthood. In adults, the symptoms of attention deficit can be reflected in career and relationship issues and sometimes in even more serious problems.

Current Treatment

The current treatment for attention deficit disorder is generally based on medication through specific drugs, and Ritalin, in particular, is widely prescribed. Very often, schools attempt to cope with these difficult children through behaviour management techniques. The children are also supported by one to one assistance, which enables them to make some progress by taking them to a quiet area, away from the other activities. Nevertheless, most children diagnosed with attention deficit, do not fulfil their educational potential.

Attention Deficit and The Turnabout Programme

Within section three of the book, we describe a series of mental games and exercises that have been successful in diminishing and alleviating the attention deficit problem. The majority of people with ADD or ADHD will be greatly assisted by the Turnabout exercises. Many of the people who have undergone the Turnabout Programme have been able to progressively reduce their drug dependency and some have been able to dispense with their medication. Reduction in medication should only be undertaken with a doctor's advice and consent.

There are some very fundamental differences in the approach taken by the Turnabout Programme, by comparison with conventional treatment. Within the programme, we are training the brain to act differently and to be better able to cope with the multitude of sensations, both within the classroom and in life outside of school. Unlike other treatments, which look just to contain the problem, the Turnabout Programme is seeking to resolve the attention deficit and enable these children to manage the pressures of the classroom, in the same way as everyone else. The Turnabout Programme can be put into practice alongside conventional treatment.

Many people with ADD and ADHD, (sometimes also with other serious behavioural, psychological and learning problems), have been successfully treated using the Turnabout Programme. In the following chapter, Harry an adult American, who had suffered throughout his life from a hyperactive attention deficit problem, tells his own story of his treatment and he describes how he felt during the process of change and the difference that it has made to his life.

The majority of children diagnosed with attention deficit problems, including children with ADHD, will be greatly helped by the exercises set out in section three. As a parent of a child with an attention deficit problem, you can commence these exercises with assurance, based on the success of other children, some with serious hyperactivity. We confidently expect that you will be able to lead and assist your own child in making this most crucial turnabout.

Attention Deficit Problems Disappear. The Story of Alan

It started out as a crisis but within the year the problems were resolved.

The parents of fourteen-year-old Alan had finally reached the stage where they felt that he needed to see a psychiatrist to be assessed. He was exhibiting attention deficit characteristics with extreme hyperactivity. Most of the time, both at school and at home, he was clowning about and acting the fool; whilst at other times he was very impulsive, over-reacting emotionally to any little incident. Now it had reached crisis level. Alan had opted out of school and was refusing to return.

Before they went to the psychiatric hospital, Alan's parents had their first meeting with Carol Goldfus. They described their despair that their only son seemed to be totally non-functional.

Alan was persuaded to give the Turnabout Programme a try and to see how things worked out. The appointment with the psychiatrist was cancelled. After his initial apprehension, Alan attended the programme regularly, three times a week and he undertook the whole of the core training programme. In particular, he was given intensive memory training.

It was very apparent that a major part of Alan's problem was his negative approach to life. To combat this attitude, he was encouraged to undertake the self-assessment process within the programme (see chapter eighteen). At the age of fourteen, he began to reflect on who he was, where he now stood in his life and where he might want to be in the future. As is usually the case, Alan's clowning around and appearing not to care or to want to try, was just a defensive barrier that he had set up to protect himself from the embarrassment of failure.

We should remember that, however it might appear to the outside world, nobody really wants to fail. During the first few months, Alan gradually began to see an improvement in his ability to learn, largely brought about by improvements in his memory. At the same time his self-confidence gradually began to emerge. As time passed, Alan stopped playing the clown and decided it was time to take himself seriously. His parents were called in, a re-assessment of the situation was made, and it was decided to enrol Alan in a new school where his previous condition was unknown.

After nine months of Turnabout training, Alan reached the point where he was able to function comfortably and successfully in the classroom. From then on, there was no thought of a need for psychiatrists or for special treatment of any sort. Now, two years later, Alan is no longer the clown; he is confident, self-sufficient and properly integrated into society.

Chapter Four

Harry's Story

Harry, a forty-four year old American engineer, was referred to the Turnabout programme when his severe attention deficit problems together with his depression, became just about too much for him to cope with.

There are a number of classic attention deficit symptoms and, unfortunately for Harry, he had a good selection of them. He was easily distracted and unable to finish jobs properly; he was highly impulsive, acting before thinking; he was disorganised and from time to time, he was more than a little aggressive and argumentative.

These symptoms were directly reflected in his troubled personal life and in his failing career. Harry's marriage of fifteen years was in the process of being dissolved. He was undergoing therapy to help manage his life in light of the loss of his wife, his home, his family and his job and his inability to motivate himself in job searches, or to function and organize himself sufficiently to survive his present life crisis.

Harry was just about getting by. He needed very high dosages of Ritalin to combat his attention deficit problems and his emotional problems were being addressed in various therapy sessions, with a number of different therapeutic techniques being attempted. But still Harry complained that his attention deficit manifestations were making it extremely difficult for him to function at all. He was then recommended to see Dr Carol Goldfus, in an attempt to deal with his ADHD related problems. Here is Harry's story in his own words.

"At the first meeting with Carol I gave her a bit of background about the situation that I found myself in. She spoke with me a bit to understand my problem, and immediately pulled out coloured bricks and cards with different shapes, which I had to reconstruct from memory. Child's play! Like a psychometric exam that I always scored well on, you'd think. Look at the picture. Put it away. Reproduce the patterns. Boy, did I feel like I was foolish and being suckered.

However, much to my surprise, I kept on getting the reconstruction of the positioning of the coloured shapes wrong. Despite good scores on all kinds of abstract reasoning tests, I kept getting relatively simple arrangements of 7 or 8 coloured bricks wrong. Nothing could have been more humiliating. And dumbfounding.

Carol, however, was unmoved. As if she anticipated this type of problem.

And there was a repeated pattern in my errors. Colour reversals. Confusion on how to organize and recall the visual field of colours and locations that I wanted to commit to memory, to put into action by arranging these damn coloured blocks. Getting confused between black and white. Trying to visually photograph the patterns, and then being unable to reproduce them reliably. Feeling overwhelmed by such a simple exercise. Getting a headache above my eyes. I wouldn't have believed it had I not been confronted by these repeated failures in exercising a simple task, and experiencing the exasperation and headaches.

"What's going on here Carol", I asked. She said we were "exercising your colour and spatial perception through these exercises, in an attempt to rewire faulty cognition." What are you talking about Carol?

"I've noticed", she said, "that many children presenting with attention deficit, have a problem similar to the one you have now. We are helping you now to make new connections in your brain, to learn, and to strategize how to solve this problem. Perceptions of colour and space are in different parts of the working brain. Something is screwing up recording and retrieval of this information".

So much stuff to me. What am I to do with this information? So we continued the exercises and I observed myself and the methods I used to remember patterns of colours and their relative locations.

What I had noticed is that I didn't really 'form a picture' of the coloured patterns in my mind's eye. Instead, as I looked at the colours, I would say them to myself and form a 'rule' for positioning the sequence of colours that I remembered. If I looked at a square of four different colours, I would start with the lower left corner and attempt to reconstruct the square by placing the 'remembered' colours in sequence according to my sub vocalized memory of the colours from this anchor position and proceeding clockwise. This strategy was frustrated when there was a more complex pattern of the coloured bricks that wouldn't enable implementation of a simple rule like 'place colours clockwise'.

And still I got these patterns wrong. But, as we continued, and I noticed the consistency of my mistakes, a new insight emerged. I would look at one colour, recognize it as that colour, but remember it sub vocally as a different colour.

Hence, though I got better at reproducing the shapes in the visual pattern, the colours I would place would be the colours I remembered, and if I used the wrong word to name the colour in my mind's ear, that's what I would put in place.

When I shared this insight with Carol, she explained to me that a lot of this has to do with defective information retrieval and suggested that a lot of my frustration may result from this difficulty. She remained insistent that such exercises would ultimately help me to 'rewire', perhaps even organically, the parts of my brain involved in such information recording and retrieval. Still so much stuff to me.

Then Carol suggested a change in the nature of the exercises. Carol formulated a new set of rules for positioning coloured bricks in a three-dimensional pattern, whose 'rules for placement' were counterintuitive to the word used. For example, 'in front' was, from my perspective, 'behind' and vice versa. She then also suggested that she use verbal clues. That I close my eyes, she would recite the colours to place, and their rules of placement, and that I reconstruct the desired patterns. I did this before proceeding to the next exercise, which was usually, but not always, an extension of the existing pattern with new elements added for me to remember and reconstruct.

At first, many of the same colour reversal problems appeared. And I was confused enough by the counterintuitive placement instructions. White and Black remained a problem. However, things began to change, all so subtly, all so slowly.

First, I got better at recalling the proper sequence of colours and their positioning according to Carol's rules, in the three dimensional pattern. It then became possible to reconstruct larger and larger complexes of coloured shapes. More importantly, I began to be able to 'visualize' the patterns required for reconstruction in my mind's eye. I would note when my 'memory fell apart', that I could get the beginning or end of a coloured sequence correctly, but the middle would become fuddled.

I shared these self-observations with Carol.

But other things began to happen as well. According both to Carol, and to others around me, I began to display greater patience with my frustrations, I became less 'reactive on the spot' to a given situation, I could hold my tongue, I was able to listen without jumping in to a conversation, and I began, almost to my surprise, to become better organized.

I labelled these manifestations of change 'collateral benefit'. I queried Carol on how on earth can you attribute changes in personality and social functioning to exercises with coloured bricks. I explained to her that nothing could possibly sound more ridiculous. Carol's response relied heavily on one of the technical metaphors of the age, 'information processing.'

Carol would say to me, "You are processing information in a parallel fashion very quickly. You are too fast for many people. And you get impatient when you have to slow down and explain to them logically how you got to a conclusion. This causes you to feel intense with frustration, and perhaps even explode from time to time. We have to work on setting up the networks that will work this information through for you, even at the expense of you feeling that you are slowing down, for you to be more effective."

From coloured brick exercises?

Gimme a break!

But then I began to think about what Carol was saying.

Stroke patients recover some function formerly processed in the brain by tissue now dead. That means that other parts of the brain pick up some of this function. A plastic transformation has taken place via learning. Think about it.

Somehow the brain demonstrates the ability to plastically transform itself and accept and develop function in areas not originally 'earmarked' for such function. Some sort of body/mind learning has taken place and been imprinted in a fashion as to make the function accessible."

Harry has now been on the Turnabout programme for about one year. His initial and very forceful scepticism about the exercises has changed to 100% commitment; he has now become a very different man. In his working life he has now set himself up as an independent consultant, his time is very heavily booked and he is very busy. He is attending job interviews and is aiming for demanding positions with high level of responsibility. Harry's usage of Ritalin has come down from what was previously an extremely high dose, to a very minimal amount and soon, it should be completely dispensed with.

"I could have committed suicide but I'm still here. Now I'm multi-tasking and I'm going strong"

Section 2

Understanding The Process of Change

Chapter Five

What are Listening Skills?

This, the second section of the book, sets out to give a straightforward explanation of the underlying malfunctions that are likely to have caused the symptoms and characteristics of dyslexia and also of attention deficit disorder. The main purpose of the five chapters in this section is to provide an understanding of the rationale of the exercises that follow, in section three.

Within this chapter, we discuss the skills of listening and, in particular, the ability to distinguish clearly between one sound and another. The more appropriate term for this function is 'auditory discrimination'. A weakness in auditory discrimination can be a contributory cause of both dyslexia and of attention deficit disorder.

We must emphasise, at the outset, that we are not attempting to address physiological hearing problems. Children whose learning difficulties are a direct result of poor physical hearing, are outside of the scope of this book. If you have any doubts at all about your child's ability to hear clearly, then you should consult your doctor immediately. Chapter fifteen gives some guidance for parents who might be uncertain, whether or not to consult a doctor about their child's hearing.

Auditory Discrimination and Dyslexia

A weakness in auditory discrimination is one of the most common causes of reading disability. The Turnabout Programme has been able to bring about a greatly improved reading ability in dyslexic people, including some who were very severely affected, just by carrying out the exercises for improving their auditory discrimination capabilities.

Effective auditory discrimination is necessary to enable the reader to differentiate between similar sounding vowels and consonants. Children with poor auditory discrimination are very often unable to properly identify sounds that are similar. They are confused by and unable to distinguish between similar sounding letters, such as "a" and "e" and "b" and "d". If children cannot instinctively differentiate one sound from another, their reading will be largely based upon guesswork and will become confused. Conventional reading practice does not address this problem.

The exercises in section three, have proved to be effective, even for children who have previously endured many years of unsuccessful schooling. Improving auditory discrimination skills can begin the process of bringing the dyslexic child back into the mainstream of school life.

Auditory Discrimination and Attention Deficit

Children with attention deficit difficulties are very likely to have a low capability for discriminating one sound from another and this might well be the main reason for their condition. A weakness in this area is the first obstacle that we must overcome, to enable these children to pay proper attention, when and where they need to. The exercises in the next section of the book that focus on improving a child's auditory discrimination capability, are the starting point on the road to rectifying the attention deficit problem.

Following Instructions

This same weakness in auditory discrimination can also prevent people from properly registering a particular voice, out of a background of other noises. Children affected in this way cannot easily comprehend instructions, either from parent or teacher, nor can they easily differentiate between similar instructions. In particular, directives that involve two separate elements can be difficult for them to carry out. An apparently simple request from the teacher, such as "Get out your new reading book and come and stand in line", can be confusing and may be too much for such children to fully register. Children with poor auditory discrimination can often be identified in the classroom, by the way that they watch and follow other children in order to try to understand what they should be doing.

Children, who cannot grasp or decipher simple instructions, can appear to be ignoring their teacher or parent. This can sometimes be taken to be laziness, naughtiness, disobedience or insolence, depending on the circumstances. But the root cause of the problem and thus the solution is within the auditory discrimination processes.

Auditory Discrimination in Everyday Life

It can be difficult for those of us who do not have a problem with auditory discrimination, to understand its implications. The capability to extract significant sounds from a background of noise, and to disregard the rest, is something that most of us do automatically. This applies when we are in a crowd, in a mainline railway station, on a bus, in a busy shopping centre or wherever. Even in these noisy environments, we can usually concentrate on one conversation and ignore the many other sounds, discussions or arguments, going on around us. Similarly, if we move to a house on a main road, we may find the traffic noise to be intrusive at first but as our brain discards the background sounds, we soon cease to be aware of the noise.

People with poor auditory discrimination, cannot separate out the important sounds and disregard the surrounding noise, either automatically or deliberately. For them, it is as if the background is constantly intruding into their consciousness.

Those who cannot properly differentiate between the many sounds that are heard, have difficulty in carrying out a wide range of activities. They are often prevented from being able to acquire the skills necessary for reading or writing, which most obviously presents an immediate barrier to functioning properly within the school or workplace. Also, such people are often unable to follow simple work instructions and thereby are precluded from many careers for which they otherwise might have been suited.

In The Beginning

The skills that underpin auditory discrimination start to be developed at birth. Within the first year of life, babies acquire the ability to distinguish and understand language. But we have found that, for many dyslexic people, there was a delay in their acquisition of language, in their early years.

For some children, there is no obvious reason for their slow linguistic development, but for others, we can see that a child's learning problems have directly resulted from a disruption to the natural processes of perceiving and interpreting sounds. When we review the family histories of dyslexic people, we often find that they had delayed speech, frequently accompanied by a minor hearing impediment at a young age, that slowed down natural language development. Indeed, this has been a recurrent theme in the background of people that have been helped by the Turnabout Programme. For others, we are aware of a family disruption that appears to have restricted the natural interaction of speech between parent and child and which adversely affected the child's auditory development

Whatever the cause, for many dyslexic people there was a delay in early childhood, of their capacity to properly distinguish sounds, one from another and to remember the spoken word. Some of these children will later enter school, still with an established auditory weakness.

In their early years within school, these children often make only very slow progress with their reading. After a few years, they may still be unable to read properly. If, by this time, their auditory capabilities are still weak, the activity of practising reading can be ineffective and also counter-productive. Children can become gradually demoralised and hostile to the whole process and they begin to despair of acquiring the reading proficiency of their classmates. Of course, not all children with delayed linguistic development in early childhood will subsequently develop long-term problems.

How the Ear Works

As a background to an understanding, both of the problem and of the solution, we set out here, a very simplistic summary of the physiology of the ear.

The ear consists of three parts; the outer ear, the middle ear and the inner ear. The middle ear itself comprises three bones and between each bone there are muscles. When sounds enter the ear, they cause the bones of the middle ear to vibrate and these sounds then get sent to the auditory section of the brain via the inner ear. *We believe that this is where the problem may start for dyslexic people.*

For some dyslexic people, it is most likely that the ears do not transmit the sounds in the correct way. Therefore, as the sounds that reach the brain are inaccurate, the response from the brain will be incorrect. A simple example of this, is the child who is unable to differentiate clearly between similar letter sounds; for instance, being unable to distinguish between separate vowel sounds such as 'e' and 'a.'

In the same way that muscles in the arm or leg can be made stronger by exercise, the route of the vibrations within the ear can be trained and strengthened. This is an important part of the theoretical basis of the Turnabout Programme.

Making A Difference

We learn to read through our senses of sight, hearing and touch; the visual, auditory and kinaesthetic senses. Significantly, it is only our sense of hearing that is located within the brain. The ears are the most important medium for the acquisition of language and for the ability to read and write. For all of us, the capability to comprehend the spoken word, underpins our ability to read and to learn. (It is important to re-emphasise, that we are discussing children who do not have a problem with the physical process of hearing.)

In order to redress auditory based learning difficulties, we need to strengthen the capacity for auditory discrimination and that is the primary objective of the exercises in chapter ten. This activity must take place before significant progress can be made with reading or writing. Educationalists use the phrase 'reading ready', for young children. Improving the auditory processes by the use of the Turnabout exercises will bring about this state of reading readiness.

Directionality Problems

There is a particular issue relating to listening skills that affects a small proportion of children diagnosed as dyslexic. This relates to what is known as 'directionality', the ability to locate and react to the source or the direction of sounds, such as 'left/right', 'behind/in-front'.

An indication of this problem can be seen when children seem to turn away from the person who is speaking to them. In the classroom, such children may appear to be looking at the wall or out of a window, instead of facing the teacher. They are instinctively turning their head in the direction that allows them to most readily perceive and receive information. Once again, we must emphasise that this matter has nothing to do with a physical hearing loss. A child who is partially deaf in one ear or who has had the hearing in an ear temporarily blocked by an illness, may also act in this way. If you suspect a hearing problem then see your doctor promptly. We are concerned here only with children who process information more accurately when it comes from one side, than when it comes from the other.

Parents can check whether or not directionality is a problem by a very simple test that, for the younger child, can be made into a fun activity. Blindfold your child and then speak first from one side of the room and then from the other. Your child must attempt to locate the source of the sound and success or otherwise, will give an indication of the degree to which your child can discern the direction. If there is no accurate location of the source or if there is only partial success then there may be a problem with directionality.

If the test indicates that your child has a problem with directionality, then you should utilise the specific exercises in chapter ten, that will help to resolve this problem.

From Drop-out to Lawyer: The Story of Yvonne

Yvonne came to the Turnabout programme when she was 14 years old and ready to drop out of school. She had severe learning disabilities in reading, writing, and mathematics and indeed, in all aspects of her schoolwork. She displayed a surly and resentful attitude in the lessons.

Outside of school, Yvonne argued constantly with her parents and appeared to be very bitter with life. She later admitted that, at the time, she felt that she had been given a raw deal and she thought herself to be both ugly and unintelligent. The onset of adolescence did not help Yvonne at all. She developed severe acne, became quite plump and, all in all, she considered herself to be a bit of a mess.

Yvonne started her Turnabout training and at first she progressed quite slowly. She began the programme with the auditory training and then moved on to the visual memory training. She made gradual improvements but it took over a year before the effort really began to make any impact at all on her schoolwork. And then, after eighteen months, there came a sudden and substantial leap forward in all areas.

After that, Yvonne's educational capabilities raced ahead. Her improved learning ability brought with it greater self confidence and Yvonne slowly returned to life. She became much more involved in school activities, she started dancing classes, and she changed her diet and gradually lost a few inches. As her marks improved so did her attitude within the classroom. Yvonne began to see the benefits of her hard work with the Turnabout Programme. At the same time she became much more outgoing and was able to develop a much more positive self-image.

Now let us jump ahead seven years, to the year 2003

Yvonne has now qualified as a lawyer and she has started working in a law practice. Early in her training, Yvonne was given a large project to provide information for a major case and after many nights burning the midnight oil, she completed it on time. Yvonne then contacted Carol Goldfus, after a gap of many years. She thanked Carol and said that only now did she realise just how important it was that she was made to work within a strict framework, without any concessions to her disability. She remembered the arguments when she thought that the Turnabout training regime was too hard but now she was thankful that she was made to confront her problems, rather than, as at school, being given the many accommodations and concessions.

In addition to her obvious academic prowess, Yvonne has become an outgoing friendly person and her optimistic character shines through. She still reinforces her improvements by returning to the Turnabout training exercises from time to time. A turnabout from failure to lawyer! It shows what can be done with the proper training and with the will to succeed.

Chapter Six

Understanding Auditory Memory

This chapter is about auditory memory, the process of recording and recalling what has been heard. The capability to memorise is, of course, an integral part of the learning process; it is self-apparent that there can be no learning without memory.

Consistent difficulty in committing things to memory and in retrieving information from memory is a common characteristic of people with dyslexia. Improvement in the auditory aspect of the memory process is an essential part of bringing people up to the level of academic performance that is warranted by their innate intelligence; the level that would be possible for them if they could only remember more of what they have been told.

The understanding of human memory is an important and interesting topic for academic research in its own right and it is currently receiving increased interest and activity. However, this book has been written to provide practical help, rather than attempting to become a theoretical discourse.

What Is Memory?

By being a little simplistic, we can explain the memory processes to an extent that is sufficient for understanding the basis of the memory training exercises in section three. The auditory memory process encompasses our capability to:

1. **understand what has been heard**
2. **retain it within our memory**
3. **and retrieve it when we need to.**

Short-term and Long-term Memory

The retention of the spoken word can be divided into a broad categorization of *short-term memory* and *long-term memory*. An illustration of retention of information in short-term memory is the process of dialling a telephone number immediately after being told it. As this number is not usually copied or transmitted into long-term memory, it is soon forgotten. Sometimes, we automatically retain this unwanted information in long-term memory, but a dyslexic person would be very unlikely to do this. For most of us, if a telephone number is considered important, we will commit it to long-term memory by repetition and practice or by some appropriate mnemonic memory aid. A dyslexic person or a person with auditory memory problems cannot do this easily and does not do so instinctively.

The Memory Process

For a dyslexic person, the problem with memory may be in any one, or indeed all three of the stages of memorising.

Stage 1. The initial comprehension process.

There may be difficulties in understanding the content and meaning of what has been heard.

Stage 2. The transfer process from short to long-term memory

Dyslexic people do not do this as an instinctive and automatic process. As a direct result, they cannot easily remember quite basic facts; they quickly forget the words of a song, and they are sometimes unable to carry out simple instructions. A low ability to remember and follow instructions is sometimes mistaken for disobedience or laziness. In the secondary school environment, young people forget homework or leave books at home or on the bus. This might make them appear foolish or absent minded, but in reality these characteristics reflect an inability to properly transfer information from short term to long-term memory.

Stage 3. The retrieval from long-term memory to usage.

Even when dyslexic people have understood what they have heard and transferred the information into long-term memory, they may still find it difficult to bring out the facts in a timely way or in a different context to how they were originally heard and recorded. An analogy can be made with the storage and retrieval procedures within modern computer software. Ideally, files of information are stored in an orderly way, using a system of logical 'folders', and retrieved fairly easily when required. Alternatively, these files may be stored haphazardly, in which case a longer search is necessary. At times, even when we search diligently, we cannot find the information we need, because we have not identified and classified it in a way that enables it to be separated from everything else. For many dyslexic people, the classification processes within the brain are not in place. The brain is unable to retrieve information in a context that is different to how it was heard and stored in the first place.

For children with dyslexia, each of these three aspects of memorising the spoken word can present an almost insurmountable problem. At the level of language development and specifically with reading, dyslexic children have difficulty in remembering letters and words. Even familiar words such as 'there' and 'where', and other simple words that they have attempted to read many times, are forgotten from one day to the next. Some children are able to understand and to store information well enough, but they have a problem when trying to retrieve it. This leads them to say such things as; "I know it in my head. It's all there, but it comes out wrong."

Auditory Memory Retraining

When we undertake the retraining of a dyslexic person, we need to focus on each of these three stages of auditory memory. Firstly, we need to work on the accuracy of the perception of stimuli, ensuring that people are able to hear the sounds of letters and of common words correctly; thus bringing about greater comprehension.

When we have made some progress with accuracy, we can then begin to emphasise the processing of these stimuli fast enough so that the information is speedily recorded and is retained.

And thirdly, we must give the dyslexic person the tools to organise the storage of information in an orderly way, so that it can be retrieved within a reasonable timescale and in the order in which it is needed.

The exercises in section three provide intensive memory training to assist a person who has memory retention problems. The Turnabout exercises are carefully structured to improve each of the three stages of the auditory memory process.

Improving comprehension

All of the memory training exercises start with a need for comprehension. Most of the exercises require the participants to listen to the instructions with their eyes closed, focusing only on listening to and comprehending the message. This is the first stage of the auditory memory process and the first element of retraining the memory.

Faster transfer from short-term to long-term memory

The memory training exercises become progressively more demanding, as they move from one stage to the next. When the information to be remembered becomes too comprehensive to be stored in the short-term memory bank, then the participant is obliged to transfer the information into long-term memory and to attempt to retain it there. The person, who has previously avoided or circumvented the need to retain information in memory, will now be practising it on a consistent basis. Speed is important, to ensure that the information does not slip away while it is being organised in long-term memory. To reflect this, the exercises are structured so that, over time, it is necessary for the brain to work progressively faster to prevent details from being lost.

Retrieval of Information From Long-term Memory

As each of the exercises proceeds, the participants are required to record and retain increasingly large volumes of information in their long-term memory. The exercises make use of all of this stored detail and they involve practice in bringing back the information in a range of different formats and sequences.

The Need for Persistence

All of the memory training exercises are designed to start at a simple level, so that a child can usually be successful at the very first attempt. In this way, we can avoid any sense of immediate failure. Children with learning difficulties are often only too familiar with an initial inability to accomplish a task and perhaps also with indications of impatience and frustration from teachers and parents. We need success at the beginning, to motivate both the child and the parent.

Parents need to be aware, from the outset, that improvements in their child's memory will be gradual. Not only that, the process of retraining the memory can be exhausting at first, often for the pupil and sometimes for the trainer. An appropriate parallel can be found with people who practise 'weight training', where the usual approach is to start with the smaller weights and gradually increase both the number of repetitions and the weight to be lifted. In a similar way, the auditory memory exercises start with simple tasks and build up in complexity and in repetition. Through this, a person can develop greater strength and stamina in the auditory memory processes. You may need good humour and determination to continue with the exercises and to make them work, particularly with a teenage child. The much-quoted sportsman's cliché of "no pain no gain" can sometimes apply in this case.

Throughout the whole of the training programme, continue to encourage your children so that they are at ease with the process. It is always better if it becomes your child's ambition to succeed, rather than your own.

If a difficult period arises, be encouraged by the record of success illustrated by the real life examples featured in this book. Many of these people started with severe memory problems and they all struggled with their training at some point. In the end, they were all able to overcome their difficulties and many have gone on to achieve academic success well beyond their original hopes and expectations.

We recommend to parents that you record details of your child's progress in a book, so that both you and your child will be able to reflect and see how far you have come. You can liken the process to climbing a mountain; if you look up and you see what is left to do, it can be daunting. But if you look back and you see how far you have risen, you become reinvigorated and realise that you have it in you to get to the top.

A Very Quick Fix: The story of Neil

Neil was typical of many dyslexic people, as he had very mixed capabilities; good at some things and extremely poor at others. For people like Neil, improvements can be made very quickly by focusing largely (but not totally) on strengthening the weaker areas.

Neil's life history gives some clues to his developmental problems. He had hearing difficulties early in life and after some years, it was found that his ears were blocked by wax. Lack of hearing at an early age can (and in his case, did) retard speech development. Following this, Neil's progress was very slow and he displayed many dyslexic characteristics. Throughout his early school years, Neil was poor at reading and his writing was very limited.

Neil was given intensive therapy at the ages of six and seven and additional help throughout his time at school. By the end of primary school, he had improved a little but he was still very slow and had a poor memory. At eleven, Neil was sent to a boarding school but could not cope with being away from home. By the age of twelve he began to read with a little fluency but his writing still displayed dyslexic characteristics, with mixed up letters and an inability to remember spelling. In contrast to his weak literacy, Neil was very strong mathematically and he had excellent numeracy skills.

When Neil started Turnabout training at the age of sixteen, he was still painfully slow with the majority of his work at school and he could not pay attention for very long. Neil was given exercises that would improve both his auditory and his visual memory. He also practised the music based auditory discrimination exercises, to help him concentrate on the teacher and be able to disregard the classroom banter. Only a short period of time was needed for the training to take effect. After just six months within the programme, Neil began achieving high grades in all subjects, not just in mathematics. He succeeded in all of his examinations.

Neil is an example of how an intelligent and potentially academic person can be held back for many years, by the residual impact of problems that arose at a very young age. Neil also exemplifies how quickly things can begin to turn around, with the proper corrective training provided by the Turnabout exercises.

Chapter Seven

Visual Processing Difficulties

This chapter is concerned with the visual senses, the various complex functions involved with seeing images, (which can be on a page, on a screen, in the street or anywhere else), and making sense of them so that they can be retained in the memory. The total scope of this activity can be summarised under the heading of 'visual processing'. A deficiency in any aspect of visual processing, is very likely to present a barrier to being able to read or to write properly.

Many of the common symptoms of dyslexia, such as mixing up letters or failing to remember letters and simple words, can be the result of weaknesses in how images are perceived. Within this chapter we will be discussing three particular visual processing deficiencies. For people with dyslexia, any or all of these problem areas may need to be addressed, if we are to enable them to read and to write. These areas of difficulty are:

Visual discrimination
The process of being able to differentiate between different shapes (such as similarly shaped letters).
Spatial relationships'
The recognition and awareness of the relative position of objects, one to another (which might be words on a page).
Figure/ground discrimination
Differentiating foreground shapes (such as letters), clearly from the background.

We must emphasise that the conditions that we are discussing here have nothing at all to do with the effectiveness of sight; they are not related to short-sightedness, long-sightedness, or to any other physiological problem. If a person's sight is physically impaired, then reading and writing can be difficult or sometimes completely impossible. Visual problems that require medical treatment are completely outside the scope of this book. The exercises described in section three, assume that there is no physical impairment and that sight is satisfactory, even if glasses need to be worn.

Visual Discrimination

Some dyslexic people have a problem with **visual discrimination,** which is characterised by difficulty in differentiating between similar shapes. Educationally, this will show itself as a problem recognising individual letters and distinguishing between similarly shaped letters, numbers and words. Children with weak visual discrimination will mix up such letters as:

b and *d*,
p and *q*,
h and *k*,
m and *n*.

A further symptom of the same problem is a confusion that can arise with number recognition. Children with visual discrimination difficulties, sometimes cannot progress beyond two digit numbers without mixing them up. When they use numbers of three digits or larger, they are likely to consistently misread them or to transpose a number (such as seeing 392 as 293). Another symptom of this weakness is the inability to differentiate between similarly shaped numbers, such as 3 and 8.

Even for children who have started to read and to recognise the different letters, a symptom of poor visual discrimination might be a failure to note the internal details of a word. These children will confuse such words as 'big' and 'beg', 'pin' and 'pen' and other words that appear similar in shape. Such children also have a tendency to reverse letters within words, such as changing 'calm' to 'clam'.

There is a particular aspect of poor visual discrimination, which is known as 'inversion of letters'; seeing letters upside down or not realising which way is correct for each letter. This is illustrated by confusion between such letters as:

u and *n*,
m and *w*.

Any of these characteristics, consistently displayed by children, will give you an indication that there is a visual discrimination weakness. Children with visual discrimination problems will not be able to read very well and, at best, their reading is likely to be slow. This weakness can be particularly demoralizing for them and they will seek to avoid reading whenever possible. The problem will rarely go away of its own accord and most children will need positive action to help them to overcome it.

We must remember that mistaking one letter for another is a normal part of learning to read for the young child and that it occurs during the natural developmental process. How then, should parents know when it is a persistent problem, rather than part of normal development? As a general guide, we can start to suspect that there is a visual discrimination difficulty, when the problem still persists after two years of normal teaching of reading. If, at this point, a child is still consistently mixing up letters of similar shape, then we need to consider taking some remedial action. Conventional reading practice, even on an intensive one to one basis, is rarely a comprehensive solution.

Spatial relationships

Some dyslexic children have a problem associated with space, with what is known as **spatial relationships**. These children are sometimes physically clumsy; they can bump into things; they can knock things over and they can drop things. This clumsiness may be due to a low ability to comprehend the position of objects in relation to each other and to the space around them. In the context of reading and writing, this weakness shows itself in a child being unable to perceive the space between words. For instance, 'I can do it' might be written as 'icandoit', which is a typical indication of a spatial relationship problem. The inability to comprehend the position of shapes, means that children cannot clearly differentiate and recognise the shapes of the letters in a word and sometimes they cannot properly pick out the letters from the background detail on the page.

With these problems to overcome and often with visual discrimination problems as well, reading cannot be other than extremely difficult. Children with a spatial problem are often unable to read at all. Many of the exercises in the next section of the book set out to improve a child's spatial awareness, either directly or as a secondary benefit from carrying out the exercise.

Figure/Ground Discrimination

In a small proportion of cases, the two visual difficulties described above may be accompanied by a low capacity for **figure/ground discrimination**. This particular weakness shows itself as a poor capability to distinguish shapes from the background on which they are set. Children with this problem cannot readily distinguish shapes on a page from the background and are not able to copy simple shapes, such as a rectangle or a circle. Often they cannot identify an individual shape when two different shapes overlap: for example, when a circle and rectangle overlap, they will say that they cannot pick out either shape.

An inability to discriminate between a foreground figure and the background has a profoundly detrimental effect on children's ability to read, as they cannot readily separate the letters from pictures and other detail on the page. When attempting to read, they are unable to clearly differentiate between one letter and another. Children with this particular problem do not like to read and sometimes cannot read at all. This is a very specific issue that affects only a small proportion of children with learning difficulties. Although it is very serious problem and can be difficult to correct, it can be addressed by the exercises for training the visual capabilities, within section three.

The Turnabout Exercises

If your child is dyslexic, it is quite likely that there is at least one aspect of visual processing that needs to be worked on. Sometimes, it can be difficult to assess which of the three problems are holding back any particular child, as the symptoms and the reading difficulties they cause, can be very similar. However, choosing the most appropriate exercises to carry out should not be a problem in practice. In all cases, you should complete those exercises that are part of the core programme. In addition, try to select those of the 'occasional' exercises that seem most applicable to your own child.

Visual perception difficulties have a detrimental effect on the fluency of reading. Overcoming this weakness will not in itself be sufficient to 'cure' dyslexia, which is much more than just how the image is perceived by the eye. But if your child has symptoms that match up to those described in this chapter, then carrying out the exercises will be an important part of the improvement process.

My Own Story by Terri, aged 16

"When I was in second grade in school, I was diagnosed as having a learning disability. At the beginning, I didn't really know what it was. All I knew was that I was different to most people. In school, I had a teacher who would help me during school time with my studies and everything that concerned my disability, which really is a problem in learning to read. I also made lots of spelling mistakes and she used to correct all my spelling mistakes. Until approximately fifth grade, she used to help me and I managed in school. After that, I had help after school with a teacher who helped me to do all my homework. This was the plan until I left elementary school. I received help from the beginning of school and I only managed because of this help.

When I came to the junior high school, this was another league. It was much more difficult and in addition, I didn't only have to worry about my disability and the fact that I couldn't read very well, but I also had a social problem. This was a new school, with new children, a new class, many teachers and the situation was frightening, despite the fact that I had friends who came with me from the elementary school. The 'after school' teacher was no longer available to help. I could not read well and I was failing. The first year at junior high was terrible. I just did not manage and felt awful. Later in the eighth grade my mother took me to Carol. At our first meeting, Carol explained to me what a learning disability really is and how I could improve my level and my ability to learn. She also explained to me that we could not ignore it and that I had to learn to cope with the disability and overcome it and that is exactly what happened.

At the beginning, she explained to me how the brain works and where my problem in the brain may be and what we could do together, to try to overcome the problems and teach me to function better in the classroom. We started with coloured bricks and the musical exercises. In the beginning I didn't like it at all, it made me very nervous and I couldn't understand what the connection was between playing with coloured bricks, with listening to music and learning in school. Although Carol explained to me that we were working on my memory, I could not see the connection. When I think back now, with the bricks and with the music, I was able to remember things better and started taking part in discussions in the class. I forgot to mention that I was a very quiet student and never raised my hand or took part in anything, as I was always afraid that I would be laughed at.

I also had many crises with Carol. Although she was supposed to help me overcome my disability, she always made me face things as they were and I wasn't always very happy. But I started improving and everything seemed to be going fairly well until Carol told the history teacher that I must do the same test as everybody else and not only do half a test. In that test I failed dismally. I received a grade of 35%. How I cried and how angry I was with Carol. I will never forget that day my mother phoned Carol and told her what had happened and I started to cry when I came for my next lesson. But Carol said, "That is life and life is not fair", and that I have to learn to manage and cope with the problem I have. She explained to me that I had actually succeeded, because I wasn't treated as somebody different but that I was treated the same as everybody else in the class. That time I scored 35% but as time would pass, she led me to understand that I would improve.

Time passed and then I had another crisis, smaller this time, in literature. I could not read a book and I was unhappy that I had never finished a proper book. But after all of the exercises and with the help of the programme, I learned to read and I actually finished my first book!

At the start of tenth grade, the beginning of high school, I started learning in the way that Carol had trained me and I saw results. My marks are now the highest in the class and I get a distinction in most of my subjects. I cannot believe it. All my life I have worked very hard and found it all very difficult when I failed. Now, almost at the end of tenth grade, I am really succeeding. To think that once I hated history and today I participate in the class and my grades are very high and most important of all, I enjoy my studies and every moment of studying is a joy to me."

Chapter Eight

Understanding Visual memory

In chapter six, we discussed the topic of auditory memory; the process of remembering what has been heard. In this chapter, we are considering visual memory; the capability to look at objects, to retain them in our memory and then retrieve the information, or recognise the same object or image when we see it again. These objects might be letters, words, numbers, events, pictures, faces, or images of any kind.

Memorising what we see is by no means a simple and straightforward matter. This is illustrated by the extremely varied accounts given to the police, by multiple witnesses who have seen exactly the same incident. As with everything else in life, there are some people who have better visual memories than others. Within this book however, we are dealing with people at the low end of the scale, and for whom a poor visual memory can be a formidable barrier to the process of learning to read.

Visual memory skills are complex. When applied to reading they represent the process of recording what is seen, making a comparison with something that has been seen before and recognising a pattern. Where this capability is lacking, the difficulties for the aspiring reader are self-evident. Children with a weak visual memory can look at common words, such as 'here' and 'there', and often be unable to recognise them, however many times they have seen them before. Sometimes, these children cannot remember all of the letters of the alphabet, or even the majority of the letters.

For dyslexic children, memory weaknesses are often a major contributory cause of their reading and writing difficulties. If a child cannot remember common words, then each time a word is encountered it has to be read phonetically, as if it has never been seen before. If the same child also cannot remember the idiosyncrasies of the spelling of many words in the English language, (the different pronunciations of 'though' and 'cough' as an example), then the ability to read fluently can never be acquired.

A visual memory deficiency, even without any other weaknesses, will be enough to ensure that every attempt at reading practice is a struggle for the child. The entire reading process is slowed down and children with a visual memory problem might eventually stop trying and become alienated from the learning process. But, be assured that memory can be strengthened and that the deficiencies can be corrected. Children can then begin to remember the words and letters that they see and hear and they can start to be able to comprehend what they read.

Sequential Memory

There is one particular aspect of the visual memory process, which when weak, shows itself in difficulties with writing. Some people are able to recognise all of the letters when they read, but when they attempt to write the words down, they are unable to accurately recall the *sequence* of the letters within the word. As indicated by the characteristics, this is known as a *sequential memory* problem. Visually received information is stored and retained by such people, but they cannot bring the information out other than in a jumbled fashion. Children with this problem will usually have a low spelling ability, as might be expected. Some of the memory training exercises are particularly targeted at assisting people to manage the sequencing mechanisms within their memory.

Memory Training

The process of training the memory to store and then to recall what has been seen is not as formidable as it might appear. All of the visual memory exercises in section three of the book are very practical and the participant usually enjoys them. Most of them can and should be treated as games. The exercises are designed and structured to encompass all aspects of the visual memory process from:

Initially viewing and recording - to

Controlling the sequence of the elements to be memorised and recording them in a structured way, in long-term memory - and then to

Reproducing information in the correct sequence.

When carrying out the memory training, please take into account the quite considerable strain that these exercises can bring about at first. The effort required in retraining the visual processes, in particular the visual memory, can sometimes be intense and exhausting. Children whose dyslexia is directly related to visual problems are prone to become very tired, even after a few minutes. You should not over-expose young children to the exercises at first. Chapter sixteen gives guidance on a gradual build-up.

The visual memory exercises use a wide range of media for training the memory, including dice, coloured bricks, pictures and many objects. If your child stalls on any one exercise or seems to find it a great strain, then leave it for a week or two and concentrate on the others. You may find that you can only carry out any one particular visual memory exercise for a few weeks and then you will need to break off and continue with the other exercises only. Should that happen, you will usually be able to return to the exercise on hold, after a pause of two or three weeks.

Attention Deficit and Visual Memory Weaknesses

In general, visual memory weaknesses are not a major cause of attention deficit problems, although there are some children with an attention deficit, who do have an issue with visual memory. If you are unsure whether or not this is a problem for your own child, you can start the exercises for improving visual processing that are in chapters thirteen and fourteen and if you find that your child is able to race through them quickly and easily, then you may chose to bypass them and concentrate on other more relevant activities.

Interaction With Auditory Memory Training

Dyslexia and other learning difficulties usually manifest themselves in poor reading and writing, and this can sometimes make it appear that visual problems are the exclusive cause. This is not necessarily or indeed usually, the case. Most often, the problems arose initially from weaknesses in a child's auditory processes and therefore, fundamental improvement has to be made through the auditory exercises. So, even if it is clear-cut that your child has the visual memory symptoms described here, the auditory exercises must not be neglected.

Improving Visual Memory: The Story Of Annie

Seventeen-year-old Annie came to the Turnabout programme as a nervous and unhappy young lady. She had been diagnosed with dyslexia and had quite a range of difficulties. These were mostly related to her reading and her inability to remember the familiar everyday words that she had viewed many hundreds of times. Somehow or other, she could not manage to fix them into her memory. As a consequence of this, her reading and writing were very limited and she could not progress with any academic subject that required her to read and to study. She had particular problems with history and could not remember facts or the chronology of events.

Annie began her Turnabout training programme and she carried out the full core training twice a week, very diligently. In particular, she was encouraged to concentrate on the exercises to improve her visual memory. As the weeks progressed, Annie found that her memory blockages occurred less frequently and that she could start to remember words when she read them and when she needed to write them down.

After just one year of training, Annie had progressed sufficiently well in school to sit her final examinations, which she was able to pass with very respectable grades. No longer did exam panic prevent her being able to function at all.

Her personality has blossomed and she is far less tense and anxious than she was when she began the training. Just twelve months after she started the Turnabout training, this young lady, who had reached the age of seventeen barely able to put two written words together, produced the following letter, properly written.

"Dear Carol

I wanted to say a few words to you. I wanted to say thank you very much from the bottom of my heart. Both of us know that this year together has helped me in many fields. Of course you did not only influence me in my study but also my morale and my feelings. In the beginning, as with all beginnings, it was quite hard but after a short time the training passed very quickly and the sessions were enjoyable. I hope that you also enjoyed the lessons together. I want to wish you all the best for the future. I hope you will give other pupils the same help that you gave me.

Annie"

Chapter Nine

The Impact of Low Self-Esteem

It is characteristic of children with dyslexia and with an attention deficit problem, that they lack self-confidence and can build up a self-image of being a failure. Within school, this is noticeable even in reception classes, where children as young as five are already able to devise strategies to avoid tasks that they find difficult. But it is a particular problem with older children, whose awareness of their lack of success is intensified by the advent of adolescence and by general teenage anxieties. A lack of self-belief often results in children applying insufficient effort and commitment to their schoolwork and, through this, the cycle of failure is reinforced. Similarly, other children try very hard, but their lack of confidence prevents them from accomplishing anything worthwhile. A low level of self-esteem is a barrier to the improvements that we want to bring about, and it must be addressed as seriously as the direct learning issues.

The Self–Perpetuating Failure

A succession of failures can become self-perpetuating; lack of success can cause children to make excuses not to try in class, to avoid doing homework and, when older, to miss classes or to lie about what they have been doing. The underlying and prevailing attitude is "*If I put in a lot of effort and work hard and then I am unable to answer a question in the classroom, or I fail to complete a project, or I do poorly in an examination, then I will feel inadequate and unhappy. So why bother?*"

This negative attitude soon leads to the self-justification of "*If I do not prepare for a test or I do not listen in class or apply myself in any way, then I am vindicated. I didn't try, I couldn't be bothered, and that is why I failed.*" This pattern of 'learned helplessness' becomes ingrained in the personality and can create a self-image of being a misfit within the school setting. In extreme cases, this can cause older children to drop out of school or to become an habitual truant.

The self-perception of failure can dominate a child's personality to such an extent that it can be disruptive to the whole family environment. Externally, the child may be brash and rebellious, may shout at parents, and may be violent, in and out of school; all or any of these outward manifestations are covering up feelings of lack of self worth. In adolescence, other negative characteristics can surface, such as loneliness, a lack of social skills and an inability to make friends. These behaviour patterns are symptomatic of many children with learning disabilities. Years of apparent failure will have instilled within them a perceived inadequacy and an embarrassment at their apparent lack of skills, compared with their contemporaries.

Both sexes can experience this alienation, but there are often differences in the reactions of boys and girls. In boys, it can frequently manifest itself in aggressive lawless behaviour or in acting the clown in the classroom. Girls may sometimes become withdrawn, weepy, volatile and distracted from reality. Television and soap operas in particular, can play a significant role in this escapism, with girls living their lives vicariously through obsessive interest in the on-screen dramas.

A child's low self-esteem cannot just be accepted. Positive feelings of self-worth and self-esteem need to be emphasised and encouraged, in order to realise the full benefits of the Turnabout exercises. But, improving children's self-esteem is not just a matter of helping to resolve problems with their education. Many talented people do not fulfil themselves in many aspects of their lives, when their self-esteem is lacking. Positive self–esteem can be the key to success in life for your children.

For younger children, just being aware of the improvement they have made, may be sufficient to restore feelings of self-worth. When young children are aware that they are starting to be able to read and write, just like everyone else, then their self-confidence can emerge very rapidly. But they will need praise and encouragement for their improvement and success, and assurance that the improvements will continue. For teenagers, things are often more complicated. Their diminished self-esteem can be deeply embedded and can be a major barrier to involvement and commitment.

The Trouble With Being a Parent

The process of rebuilding self-esteem almost invariably impacts on the family as a whole. Even within the most caring and supportive family, there can be nuances that influence the self-image of a child in a negative way. Innocent and well-meaning comments can trigger the avoidance of effort, bringing about the situation whereby children do not try, so that they cannot be seen to have failed. In conjunction with an unsuccessful school career, these influences can gradually sap the confidence of a child and contribute to feelings of alienation. As parents, we sometimes have to examine our own attitudes and approach to the family and make changes in the way that we communicate with our children.

All families care for their children and intend to be supportive but we wish to highlight some common situations that may impact upon one or more children in the family, in a negative way. If you recognise one of these family scenarios as a reflection of your own, then even by making small shifts in approach, you can begin to bring about changes for the better.

Sibling Rivalry - It is quite usual for one child in the family to be less successful in school than other brothers or sisters. This can be an uncomfortable experience for the one who is not matching up to the perceived family expectations. Family pressures, even if unspoken, can cause the less successful child to circumvent any direct comparisons by not trying very hard, and sometimes quite overtly being seen not to make any effort. There are also children who are more introverted than their siblings and can handicap themselves with a self-perception of inadequacy, despite the encouragement of their parents.

Sibling Protection - Sometimes, a very well meaning older sibling will attempt to support and protect younger brothers or sisters by speaking on their behalf and asking and answering questions for them. As a consequence, the younger children may rarely need to provide information or sustain a conversation for themselves. More often than not, it is an articulate and self-confident older sister 'protecting' a brother, who is a year or two younger. Some children will resent and resist this interference, but for those who are more passive, this loving support can be greatly detrimental. Natural development can be set back, particularly language development and this may well have educational implications. A child protected in this way for some years, is usually low in self-confidence.

Parental protection mechanism - Parents will sometimes develop a protection mechanism for themselves, against the perceived stigma of a child who is not academically successful. "*My John likes to play football but he's not the studious type.*" This becomes a self-fulfilling statement. John does not see himself as succeeding in school and so does not work as hard as his classmates; he thus fulfils the prediction, and the cycle of failure is reinforced. Sometimes, parents do not recognise a situation in which their child has the potential to succeed, but needs sustained help over a period of time, before this can happen.

The ambitious parents - There are successful ambitious parents, perhaps with professional occupations, who can react aggressively or with apparent disappointment, to children who do not do well enough at school to match their own wishes or expectations. These children can be seen as not trying or as not working hard enough. Outspoken criticism can bring about pressure and resentment, which in itself may prevent the child from trying too hard. Sometimes, unfulfilled parental expectations can lower a child's self respect and can generate resentment and a lack of will to succeed.

These relationships within the family environment can make their own contribution to the loss of self-esteem. All parents mean well for their children, but it is worth reflecting for a few moments, whether or not there are any undercurrents within your own family that could be generating a reluctance by your child to try as hard as others, to succeed.

Peer pressure - In the last few years, a culture has developed, in which it is 'cool', not to be seen to be trying too hard at school. Children may be failing in school, but the attitudes of their school friends can still make them seem quite content with life. Such children may gain peer approval through outward defiance of the teaching establishment or by sporting prowess or by whatever might appeal to or amuse their friends. Usually, an underlying lack of self-confidence is concealed by this bravado. The situation is not easy to combat and it needs the support and resilience of the home to enable your child to stand out against the crowd.

The importance of maintaining the self-esteem of your children is emphasised throughout this book and advice and guidance on re-building self-esteem is the basis of chapter eighteen. Throughout the time your child is carrying out the exercises, continue to give encouragement and support. Equally crucial, is that you should not give any outward show of impatience or exasperation, when a particular stage of an exercise is proving to be difficult. We also recommend, that during the time that you are implementing the programme, you keep a record of the progress of your child, so that by seeing how far you have come, both you and your child can have renewed optimism.

There is a symbiotic relationship between success and self-esteem. As children develop through the Turnabout exercises and as they begin to realise that they are progressing towards proper reading and writing, they become happier and more secure as young people. And, in the other direction, improved self-esteem can bring about a more confident and determined approach to the Turnabout Programme, which accelerates the ability to accomplish the exercises.

All children undertaking the Turnabout Programme will need to make a sustained effort, particularly those more severely affected. They will need encouragement and endorsement by their family to help them to remain motivated and to recognise that the effort will indeed be worthwhile and that they have, within themselves, the capacity and potential to succeed.

Section 3

The Turnabout Exercises

Chapter Ten

Exercises to Improve Listening Skills

Introduction to Section Three

This, the third section of the book, describes the exercises within the Turnabout Programme. There are five chapters in this section, which between them contain fifteen mental exercises, some with several phases. Each exercise is targeted at one or more of the underlying causes of dyslexia and of attention deficit disorder, but not all of the exercises will be applicable to any particular person. Most of the exercises can and should be treated as games.

Some exercises are designated as 'core' exercises; we recommend that these be carried out regularly and consistently or as a necessary pre-curser to other exercises. The core exercises are those numbered:

10/1, 10/2, 10/3, 11/1, 11/2, 12/1,13/1, 13/2, 13/3, 14/3.

Other exercises are described as 'occasional', and as the description suggests, they can be used from time to time. Nonetheless, these occasional exercises can make a major contribution to the Turnabout.

The Turnabout Programme can be administered by many people, including parents, grandparents, other family members, teachers, and friends of non-reading adults. But, for the purpose of this book, we have described all of the exercises, as if we are directly addressing the parents.

The Focus of Attention

The main objective of this chapter is to help people to develop and control their listening skills; the more technical term for this capability is 'auditory discrimination'. The underlying problems for people with a weakness in their capacity for auditory discrimination are described in chapter five.

This chapter introduces exercises based on music. People who have developed the ability to differentiate between sounds, by listening to music, have subsequently become more aware of all other types of auditory input, including the sound of individual letters, sequences of letters and of words. By using these music-based exercises, a weakness in auditory discrimination can be reduced and progressively eliminated.

Introducing The Musical Exercises

The exercises are straightforward to understand and to carry out, but they can be quite rigorous for children with learning difficulties. At the start, children should not be coerced into doing more than they can cope with and enjoy. Some children may show signs of antagonism initially as the exercises begin to confront the essence of their problems.

A consequence of using music in this way is that the resentment and disenchantment that some children may have displayed in the classroom, slowly dissipates. The very personal responses which children make to music will sometimes encourage them to 'open up' and they are able to express themselves through a medium which is less threatening than the printed word.

It is generally preferable that classical music be used for the exercises that follow. Our experience with pop music in this context has not been as satisfactory and therefore it is recommended that modern popular music be used very sparingly. However, if your child's resistance to classical music is great, you can start by using some popular music that the child can relate to and then move on to classical music as quickly as you are able.

The availability of suitable music should not present a major barrier to any parent, even those without a collection of classical CD's. Most record stores have a selection of CD's that contain excerpts from well known pieces of classical music. A table of suggested music for use with each of the exercises is shown at the end of the chapter.

Exercise 10/1: Listening to Music

Introduction

This first exercise represents a comfortable and relaxed start, with no measures of success or failure. All you need to do is to ask your child to listen to a piece of music and then you help and encourage your child to identify sounds that are *different to each other.* It is the beginning of the process of improving auditory discrimination, by differentiating between sounds. The task may seem simplistic but some children with learning difficulties have a very low capability in this area, and even this straightforward starting point is not easy for them. In view of this, it is essential that children are encouraged to feel that they are free from any pressure or tension.

This activity is usually necessary for the younger child, but for the teenager you may decide to bypass it or only use it as a brief introduction to the exercises that follow.

To Start

The procedure is to play music to children and as they are listening, you make them aware of sounds that are *dissimilar,* one to another, such as:

- *Dissimilar by the different sound of each instrument*
- *Dissimilar by the range of sound each instrument can make*
- *Dissimilar by volume*
- *Dissimilar by being a single instrument or several instruments of the same type (e.g. a violin solo a string quartet).*

Start by playing music that has a clear-cut distinction between two instruments, such as the piano and the orchestra, or between a violin and the piano. Identify the instruments that are being played. You can gradually vary the music, so that your child is being obliged to differentiate between many different sounding instruments, such as a guitar, the piano, trumpets, violins or any other clearly defined instrument.

When you start the process of listening to music in this way, do so for only about five minutes at a time and two or to three times a week. It should be a pleasant and relaxing activity for children, who must not feel that they are back in the classroom.

The table at the end of the chapter gives some suggestions for suitable music.

Continuation - The Development of Rhythm

One of the objectives of the musical exercises is to bring about an enhanced rhythmic capability. To do this you need to continue to play music to your children and encourage them to *clap to the beat or the rhythm* or to tap it out with their hands onto a table. Waltz music or any music with a repetitive beat is suitable for this activity.

In English primary schools, teaching rhythm is part of the curriculum, but the dyslexic child will usually need more practice than is given in schools. Many children with dyslexia have not developed a sense of rhythm. They cannot feel or identify the beat of the music; for example they cannot grasp the 1,2,3 rhythm of the waltz. By encouraging and developing this rhythmic sense, we will be making the child ready for the next exercise, which is largely based on a comprehension of rhythm.

Outcome

Very often, this is the first Turnabout exercise undertaken by dyslexic children, some of whom have had years of failure and discouragement. There should be no measurements of achievement or of any rate of progress. There is no success or failure in sitting and listening to different instruments. Just try to listen to the music together with your child and in a relaxed way.

After a period of time, children become more able to hear and to tap out the rhythm. As they become able to do this more easily, they are then ready to advance through the music-based training that follows.

Exercise 10/2: Introducing The Figure Of Eight

Introduction

This important exercise is the start of the process of developing auditory discrimination, through the use of music. The exercise works by requiring the participant to listen carefully for tunes, themes, and different instruments. It brings about an improved sense of rhythm and encourages greater powers of concentration, through careful listening and the need to translate the sounds onto paper.

For some children, with the more extreme dyslexic symptoms, this exercise has been the only way to start the process of improving their auditory capability.

To Start

1. In this exercise, you play music for your child to listen to and at the same time, your child should draw a representation of the music, on to paper. Your child should be presented with a large sheet of blank unlined paper, laid out flat onto a table; the younger the child, the larger the sheet of paper that should be used. For a young child, a sheet of paper about two feet by eighteen inches, is about right. The paper should be placed horizontally not vertically, so that the child can draw from left to right or from right to left. As a first step, children should be encouraged to draw, to write or to scribble, while the music is playing. They can write down anything they want to do, or are able to do. This activity should continue for a few minutes, perhaps five minutes or so.
2. Children should be encouraged to draw to the music without any constraints. Continue this for the first five or six times the exercise is done. After that, the exercise proper commences.
3. At this point, your child should be encouraged to draw shapes to match the rhythm of the music. At first, children can draw whatever shapes or patterns or scribbles they wish, as long as they move the pencil in time to the music.
4. After a few times of drawing anything at all, you should encourage your child to draw lines in time to the music. The lines can be up

and down or across the page or whatever shape your child feels is matching the flow and rhythm of the music.

Waltz music is ideal for starting this exercise, with its easily identified beat and it's repetition. A lovely piece to begin with is Waltz Number 2 by Shostakovitz, but any waltz is fine. In particular, we have found that waltzes by Strauss are easy to use and are enjoyed by most children.

Continuation - The Horizontal Figure of Eight

1. After some repetitions, the lines that children draw in time to the music will usually start to evolve into swirling circular shapes. The objective of this next phase of the exercise is to encourage your child to develop this swirl into a shape that is similar to a *horizontal figure of eight*. The figure of eight is a crucial part of the exercise.

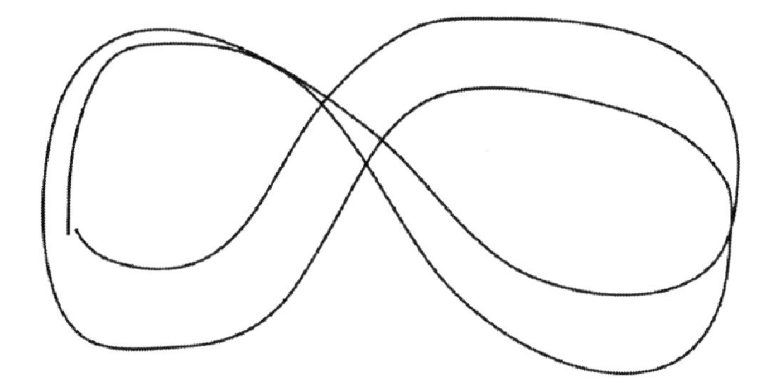

2. At first, you should try to allow this figure of eight to emerge naturally and resist the temptation to tell your child what you are expecting. Forming the horizontal figure eight is an essential component of this exercise. If this shape does not emerge as a matter of course after a few weeks, then your child should be guided to produce the figure of eight shape and encouraged to extend the drawing from one side of the page, all the way across to the other. Usually, and with patience, children begin independently to interpret the music by drawing the figure of eight shapes in time to the music.

3. If, even with parental guidance, these figures of eight do not appear on the paper, assist your child to make the figure of eight shapes in the air, by moving both hands in circles in time to the music, making sure that the hands cross over in the middle across the body. In this way you are involving both the right and left hemispheres of the brain. When you have done this for a few days, then attempt to transfer the movements and the shape onto the paper. Eventually, your child should be able to fill the whole page by drawing figures of eight on their side.
4. Encourage your child to draw thicker lines, as the music gets louder, and thinner and fainter lines when the music is soft or quiet, or alternatively to press harder or softer on the paper, depending on the loudness and intensity of the music.

The exercise of listening to the music and drawing figures of eight should continue until your child is in control and is regularly drawing the figures of eight across the whole page. In most cases, it does not take very long to master, usually about two to three sessions, but every child is an individual and what is easy for one can be more difficult for another. Some examples of how the continuous figures of eight might look are shown in the diagrams that follow. But, all children will draw something different and all will make progress at their own pace. A minute or two of drawing figures of eight on one sheet of paper will produce an untidy looking result, but this does not matter.

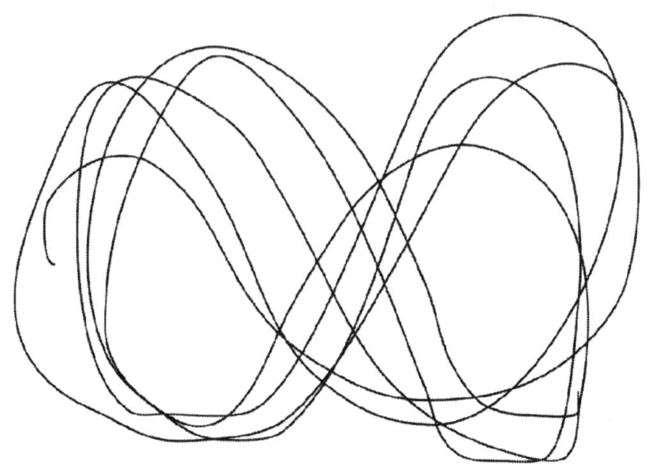

It is quite common for older children to feel awkward and uncomfortable when they are drawing to music. If, at the start, children react with nervousness or hostility, it is best to encourage them to just 'flow' and let them do whatever it is that they can and want to do, but in time to the music. The aim is to 'let go', to help children to open up and not be inhibited. Drawing to the music is usually a pleasant and relaxing experience, as soon as children become used to it and are comfortable with it.

Carry out this activity, two or three times a week, for five to ten minutes at a time. Use two or three different pieces of music each session or just the one piece if your child continues to enjoy it.

If it is easier for you, these activities with music can be done with all of the children in your family, irrespective of whether or not they have learning difficulties, so that a child with dyslexia or ADHD does not stand out from the rest.

Outcome

- ♫ This exercise utilises all three aspects of the learning process together; the auditory, by the need to listen with care and attempt to comprehend the flow of the music; the visual, by the need to see what is being drawn out and the tactile, by the act of drawing. For those who need it, it also enhances the ability to hold a pen or pencil in the right way so that the hand does not get tired.
- ♫ For some children, this exercise is a first step in their ability to be able to carry out two or more activities concurrently, through the necessity to listen to the music with care and to draw at the same time.
- ♫ The horizontal figure of eight, crossing over from left to right on the paper, is very significant. It sets up new links and connections between the right and left hand sides of the brain. For most children the results are beneficial and sometimes the impact can be quite dramatic. Many children, seriously affected with dyslexia or ADHD, have improved their auditory discrimination, directly through this exercise.
- ♫ Within the exercise, the child is listening to, absorbing and responding to the rhythm of the music as well as the tone and the volume. All languages have a spoken rhythm of their own and a

feel for the rhythm of the language is an important element of the fluent reading process.

♫ Some children with severe symptoms have demonstrated quite rapid improvements, in such matters as: listening to instructions, i.e. the music/the tone; differentiating - between louder and softer and co-ordinating the eye and hand.

Exercise 10/3: Foreground and Background Plotting.

Introduction

This third stage in the sequence of exercises of listening and reacting to music has the most substantial and effective impact. Commence it when your child has begun to feel comfortable with the process of drawing the figures of eight.

To Start

This exercise evolves naturally from the previous one. It is carried out in a similar way, by drawing the horizontal figure of eight in time to the music. This time, however, we are adding an additional dimension. The plotting is restricted to either:

the singing voice/ the main tune/ the main musical theme ***only***,

or to

the accompaniment/background theme ***only***.

Begin, with your child drawing to the voice or the foreground music. If there is no voice within the music, your child should plot the main tune or predominant theme and try to ignore the background music. The figure of eight should be drawn across the page in time to the music.

This may not be very different from what has been done in the previous exercise; except in this case the child may have to listen more carefully, to be sure that it is only the foreground music that is being drawn. (As a starting point, the music of Emma Shapplin, Carmine Meo, works well for this exercise.)

Continuation

♫ The particular feature of the exercise is this second phase, when the child is required to listen to and to plot *the background theme or accompaniment* within the music. Much music has a very clear definition between the foreground music, which might be the main tune, the voice or the soloist and background or accompanying theme being played by other musicians. Suggestions of suitable music to use for this exercise are given at the end of this chapter.

♫ Picking out the background theme of the music is often not easy for the child. As a first step in listening for the accompaniment, part of the exercise (about two minutes) can be 'drawing' the sound of the bass or trying to plot on paper just the sound and rhythm of the drums. If your child finds this difficult at first, the rhythm of the accompaniment, in particular the drums, can be banged onto the table. Later, the sounds of the drums can be created on paper, in whatever shape the child produces.

♫ At first, the child, who has mastered the process of isolating and drawing out the main theme, might still find it difficult to discern the background theme and set it down on paper. If your child has these initial difficulties and is not able to interpret the background music, restrict this exercise to plotting on paper the main musical theme and afterwards, tapping out onto a table the rhythm of the background or accompaniment. You may need to continue the process of 'banging out' the background rhythm, for some weeks, until eventually your child is capable of making a good attempt at plotting out the background music on to paper.

♫ In due course, the background/accompaniment needs to be plotted using the horizontal figure of eight, stretching out from right to left or from left to right. Do not worry too much about the figure of eight at first. When your child starts to plot the accompaniment, whatever is drawn and whatever comes out, is acceptable. But do not allow this to continue for too long. The real benefit to your child will come when the figure of eight is being drawn across the page, in time to both the foreground theme and then separately, in time to the background accompaniment.

♫ The drawing can be done either using separate sheets of paper for the foreground and the background sounds or alternatively and preferably, using two colours on the one sheet; one colour for the foreground and the other for the background. Try to keep to a consistent colour theme as you continue with this exercise; such as red for the foreground music or main theme and blue for the background music.

♫ Even when children are familiar with this exercise, the drawings often appear untidy and sometimes they may spread to many pages. In most cases, the drawings gradually become more structured, and shapes resembling the horizontal figure of eight become predominant, for both the foreground and background music.

♫ With these musical exercises, as for the other exercises in the book, you need to try to strike a balance. You must allow sufficient time for the process to work and do what it is designed to do, but the activity must not be so intensive that your child develops an aversion to it. On each occasion, the exercises should be carried on for a minimum of five minutes and for up to fifteen minutes, if your child is continuing to enjoy the music. This is an excellent exercise, with far reaching benefits. Try to carry it out two or three times a week.

♫ Notwithstanding the inclinations of your child, the majority of current pop music, with its heavy and repetitious beat, is unsuitable for use with this exercise. If your own teenage child is hostile to classical music, then perhaps you can make a deal, "one of yours to one of mine". If you have to use pop music, the heavy musical beat is usually too simplistic, but isolating the electrical guitar from the drums is sometimes not an easy task and that can be used for this exercise. Many teenagers enjoy 'drumming out' the bass and some children, who have developed through these exercises, have gone on to learning and playing the drums.

♫ Occasionally, it can be beneficial to carry out each of the musical exercises using one single headphone. This should be placed the right side of the head. The right ear allows information to go to the left hemisphere of the brain, which is responsible for language.

Outcome

Improved Auditory Discrimination – All of the benefits described for the previous phase of the exercise, will be extended by this more demanding variant. The effect of practice with this and the two preceding musical exercises is to improve an individual's capability for accurate auditory discrimination. Children are obliged to discriminate between many different instruments and focus on a wide range of themes and interactions between foreground and background music.

Multi-tasking Ability - By drawing instinctively, at the same time as listening to the music, children will have been trained to carry out two activities simultaneously, which previously they may have found to be very difficult. As children begin to 'multi-task' in this limited way, their newly developed capability will be carried forward into other aspects of their lives.

Attention Deficit – For children with attention deficit disorder, the musical exercises can be very effective. The exercises develop strengths that enable these children to be able to concentrate on important matters more readily and instinctively and be able to disregard the background and less significant sensations.

Exercise 10/4: Addressing Directionality Problems

Introduction

This exercise is appropriate only if you have carried out the tests for the symptoms of directionality (see chapter five) and you believe that your child has this particular problem. If that is the case, you should carry out each of the two previous exercises in this chapter, but for some of the time *using headphones.*

To Start

When your child is listening to the music and drawing the figures of eight, play the music through a single headphone for part of the time and mostly through the less effective ear.

Outcome

By concentrating much more on the less sensitive side and by forcing the auditory processes to work through the weaker ear, you will strengthen the capability of the weaker side to receive information and to comprehend it.

What Music To Use

You don't need to be a music expert or enthusiast, to carry out the musical training described in this chapter. As long as you have a good enough musical 'ear' to identify the different instruments, such as violins, trumpets and others, you will be able to manage perfectly well. It is not too difficult to find pieces of classical music that provide opportunities for differentiating the foreground theme from the background. Music by Mozart usually gives a clear discrimination between foreground and background, but some teenagers tend to find it rather slow and boring, so you may not be able to continue with it for too long. Much 'gypsy' music is a very effective, with bold guitars standing out clearly from the background.

For the teenage child who is struggling to discriminate between foreground and background sounds, some jazz is very suitable, particularly New Orleans type traditional jazz, with its distinctive pattern of foreground tune and separate background rhythm section. There are some excellent reproductions of early jazz, played by Louis Armstrong and others, which readily enable the tune and the accompaniment to be separated and plotted onto paper.

Music is often integral to the lifestyle and self-image of teenage children and it can sometimes be difficult to deal with them in matters relating to it. If, in the end, you can only persuade your children to carry out these exercises with music of their own taste, then at least give them the task of trying to tease out the sounds of different instruments; the drums, guitars etc. If you find yourself having to use pop music because of resistance to all other types, then it is better to do this, than to completely miss the opportunity for improving your child's auditory capability. Listening to pop music still obliges your child to do two things at once; to listen and to write or to listen and to beat in time and it can provide some limited auditory training for the dyslexic child. With a reluctant teenager you can gradually introduce different forms of music and encourage your child to try out music that is not currently fashionable. Sometimes, music from the movies can be a bridge; both acceptable to the teenager and effective for these exercises.

There is a wide range of music that is suitable for each of the exercises in this chapter. The following lists of suggested pieces of music for each exercise, contain only music that is available on compendiums of popular excerpts of classical music.

Separating the Instruments (Exercise 10/1)

Any piece of music is suitable that has a small number of instruments, or with each instrument clearly defined. Such as:

Britten	Young Persons Guide to the Orchestra
Tchaikovsky	Chinese Dance
Tchaikovsky	Dance of the Sugar Plum Fairy
Prokofiev	Montagues and Capulets from Romeo and Juliet
Purcell	Trumpet voluntary

Drawing Figures Of Eight (Exercise 10/2)

Any waltz is suitable to start and to continue with. Some of the pieces of music set down below are waltzes; others have a very different tempo and will give variation and interest.

Falla	Ritual Fire Dance
Dvorak	Slavonic Dance in C major op 46/1
Khachaturian	Waltz from Masquerade
Khachaturian	Sabre Dance
Tchaikovsky	Russian Dance
Vaughan Williams	Fantasia on Greensleeves
Elgar	Chanson de Matin
Rimsky Korsakov	Flight of the Bumble Bee
Delibes	Waltz from Coppelia
Waldteufel	The Skaters waltz

Separate Foreground/ Background Themes (Exercise 10/3)

Khachaturian	Sabre Dance
Handel	Arrival of the Queen of Sheba
Ravel	Bolero
Grieg	Hall of the Mountain King, Peer Gynt Suite
Bizet	Chanson Boheme from Carmen
Holst	Jupiter from the Planets
Rossini	Overture to The Thieving Magpie
Rodrigo	Concerto de Aranjuez
Beethoven	Turkish March

Waldteufel The Skater's waltz

Extending The Benefits

Each of the exercises will be made more interesting, if you introduce some variety; by changing the music, changing the instruments, introducing songs accompanied by piano, whatever variation that your child is willing and able to sit down and listen to and perhaps, to enjoy. Non-orchestral classical music, e.g. quartets or quintets, has great scope for improving auditory discrimination as the sounds are rarely harsh and the listener is obliged to differentiate between the few different instruments and the pitch. (This may also be the beginning of a lifetime enjoyment of this type of music.)

Alternatively, the same pieces of music can be used over and over again. Familiarity with individual pieces of music improves the child's competence in paying attention to detail.

Many children and adolescents with dyslexia can become 'closed in' and limited in their knowledge of the world, due to their difficulties with reading. We have found that musical exercises can begin to open up a wider comprehension of the world around, by providing a range of new experiences and concepts. These musical activities can sometimes be a starting point for discussion, even if the music is very unfamiliar.

The musical exercises can be returned to from time to time, as a way of reinforcing the improvements that have been made. Carrying out these musical activities invariably has a calming effect and makes children more at ease with themselves. The exercises can be returned to at any point. Use them when your child feels that coping with school is difficult, is reacting badly to the stresses of life or seems to be under pressure for no apparent reason.

The Story of Jamie - Drawing to Music

By the time Jamie reached the age of fifteen, he had been excluded from school for several months, due to his erratic and unstable behaviour and his total incapacity to see the need to conform to any of the rules. Jamie had only very minimal reading and writing capability and had been diagnosed as having ADHD.

Like many participants in the Turnabout Programme, Jamie started his training with the music-based activities, as set out in this chapter. In parallel with these he began the exercises to improve his visual learning capability.

The musical exercises required him to draw patterns to the rhythm and flow of the music and for Jamie, it was the first time in his life that he had ever drawn at all. As he carried out the musical training exercises, Jamie's drawings gradually evolved from a childlike scribble into clear distinct lines. After a few weeks, Jamie started to draw properly for the first time in his life. His drawing became increasingly important to him and when he went home, he would continue listening to music and he would draw at the same time.

Within a few months, Jamie was admitted back to school. Even after this relatively short time, his reading and writing competence had improved sufficiently for him to cope with normal school work. His erratic behaviour had diminished and much to the surprise of his teachers, he was able to sit still in class and participate in the lessons. Gradually, as Jamie became more involved with his studies, he started to be more ambitious and interested in being successful and at the same time, he continued to draw, more and more.

By the time Jamie left school, two years later, he had completely overcome his attention deficit tendencies. He was able to control his impulsivity and he had greatly improved his ability to concentrate. He passed his examinations with high grades. The teachers and school inspectors could scarcely believe his improvement, across all subjects.

But there is a real bonus for Jamie. By drawing to music, he has revealed a previously unsuspected artistic talent. He has gone on to study calligraphy, photography and art and is planning a career as a commercial artist and photographer. By undertaking the Turnabout Programme, by carrying out the musical exercises and in particular by concentrating on the process of drawing to music, Jamie has made a fundamental change to his life and to his prospects for a worthwhile career.

Chapter Eleven

Exercises to Develop Auditory Memory

This chapter contains a description of two exercises that are designed to help people to overcome weaknesses in their auditory memory and through this, be able to remember more of the detail of what they have heard.

Many dyslexic people have had problems all of their life with the ability to remember what they have been told. The symptoms may have manifested themselves in a number of ways but, very often, problems with auditory memory have been a major cause of learning difficulties in school and elsewhere.

The exercises in this chapter fall into the category of 'deceptively simple' and they are easy to comprehend and to carry out. Nonetheless, both are powerful and effective tools for improving the memory. They progress from an easy start to more demanding tasks. Both exercises have a number of distinct phases, each of a greater level of complexity than the one before. As the memory improves, the exercises continue to remain sufficiently demanding and in this way, the improvement is sustained.

As a general guide, for most people it may take a period of around three months, before the exercises bring about a noticeable change. When they do take effect, the improvements will enable people to remember more accurately and confidently and to speed up their thinking processes. Some people will make progress more quickly and others will need to persevere for longer, before effective memory processes start to become established.

For children with dyslexia, these exercises are likely to be difficult at first. Do not hesitate to go back a stage if your child seems to have regressed and cannot do this week what seemed easy enough last week. Two steps forward and then one step back is a natural part of the learning process. That same principle also applies to the exercises in the following three chapters.

The first exercise in this chapter uses dice and the other uses children's coloured bricks. Some dyslexic children can have problems sorting the dice and, for example, differentiating between the four and five spots on the dice. For these children, the apparently simple task of counting the spots and selecting and placing the dice, may be a little too much to cope with, at first. If so, they should bypass exercise 11/1, which uses dice, and go straight to exercise 11/2, which is based on the coloured bricks. Children who start with the coloured bricks, should still attempt the dice exercise from time to time and persevere until they are able to do both of the exercises. For all children, you should aim to intersperse the exercise using the dice with that using the coloured bricks.

Both of the exercises in this chapter are core exercises and should be carried out by children with dyslexic characteristics and also by those with ADD/ADHD.

Exercise 11/1: Remembering Number patterns

Introduction

This is a memory training exercise requiring children to remember simple number sequences. It uses the number patterns on dice to train and strengthen the auditory memory. To carry it out, you will need to acquire a quantity of around ten dice; these being conventional six sided dice. Preferably the dice should be larger than the very small dice that are included with some children's games. Sets of dice can usually be bought, at no great cost, from shops that sell toys or that specialises in teenage/ adult 'war games'.

To Start

The procedure is for children to listen to the spoken instruction, which is a sequence or pattern of numbers and then attempt to reproduce exactly what has been heard, using the dice.

1. Your child's eyes must be closed while listening to the instructions.
2. You start the exercise by saying to your child a sequence of numbers, (such as: one - three- four).

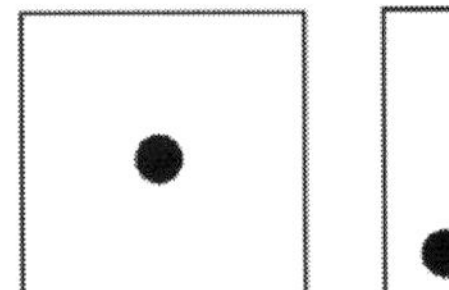 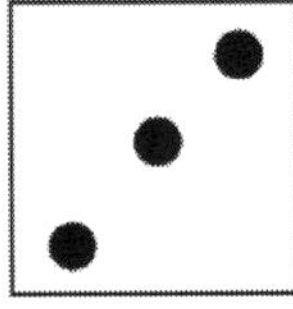 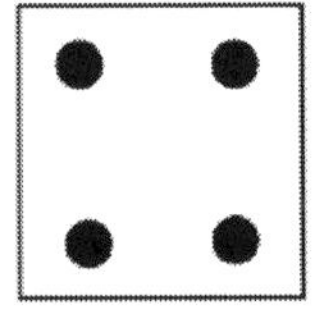

3. You then repeat again the same number sequence.
4. Now with eyes open, your child has to select and lay out the dice in a horizontal line, in the sequence you have said.
5. The dice must be put down with the number selected facing upwards as shown in the diagram below.
6. A number can be repeated in the sequence, which could be, for example: Two – five – one – five.

The recommended starting point is three numbers in a horizontal line. Most children can manage this easily, but some will finds it a little too hard at first, in which case, start with only two numbers. After some practice, your child should quickly be able to build up to memorising and recreating a four number sequence of dice.

Continue to repeat this exercise for a few minutes, around three times a week and until your child can remember the four number sequence and reproduce it on a consistent basis.

Continuation One: Above and Below

Move on to this next stage, when your child has been able to memorize and to recreate a sequence of four dice. The continuation of the exercise introduces a two dimensional aspect. In this case there is a horizontal line of dice with additional dice laid flat, *above* and *below* this line.

Each of these variations and each extra die, will gradually increase the complexity of the task. The added dimension of one die 'above' the horizontal line of dice, can sometimes be a step too soon for a dyslexic child. If, when you first try, it cannot be done at all, then go back to repeating the first part of the exercise and attempt this two dimensional task, a week or two later. But you will need to return to this 'above and below' phase of the exercise and persist with it until your child becomes able to do it fairly readily.

Explain to your child the particular configuration of dice in this exercise, with the dice above and below the line. As your child is able, work your way through each of the stages of the exercise. The variations set out below may take some weeks or months to master.

1. Remembering four and then five numbers in a row, with another die above or below, (such as: five – six – two –four – three - with a four above the two).

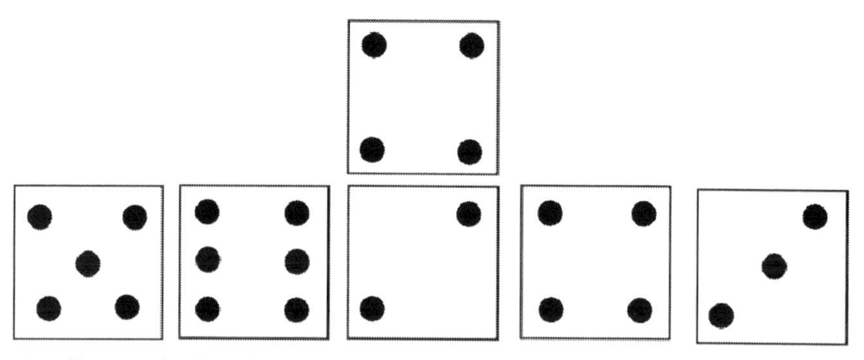

2. Remembering four numbers in a row, with two others above/ below, (such as: two – five – one – six, with a four above the two and a one below the six).

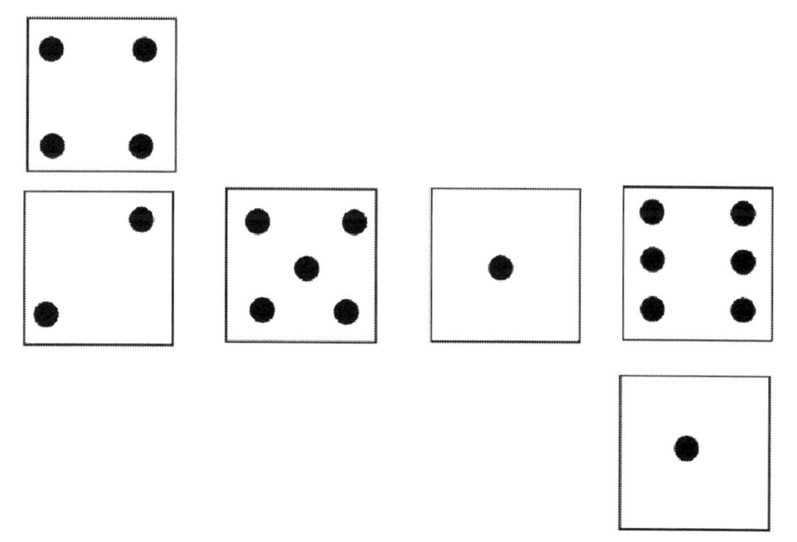

3. Five numbers in a row, with two more above/below.

4. Four numbers in a row with three more above/below, (such as: two – five – one – six, with a three above the two, a four above the five and a five above the six).

For all variations of this exercise, the same principles apply as before. Your child's eyes should be closed when listening, and you say the arrangement of dice twice, each time slowly and clearly. Now with eyes open, your child has to lay the dice flat on the table, with the selected numbers facing upwards.

Continuation Two: In front/behind

This continuation of the exercise introduces the concept of a die in front of and/or behind the others, all in one horizontal line. This is effectively extending the horizontal line, either side, by the 'in front' and 'behind' dice. This is a step up in complexity for some children as it represents a more demanding memory task than the simple straight-line sequence. For some children, each of the progressions set out below may need to be tried and repeated for a few weeks, until they can manage to remember and reproduce the more complex arrangements.

Explain to your child the way the dice are to be put down and what is meant by – 'in front' and 'behind'. Progressively work through the variations of dice in front of or behind the row, as outlined below.

1. Attempting to remember four numbers in a row, with a designated number to be placed in front of the other numbers, (such as: two – five – four – three, with a six in front of the two).

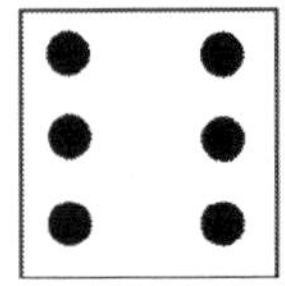 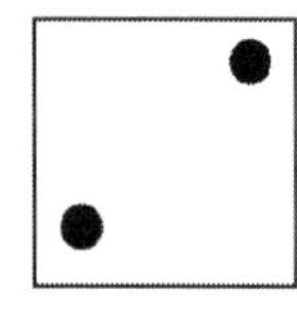 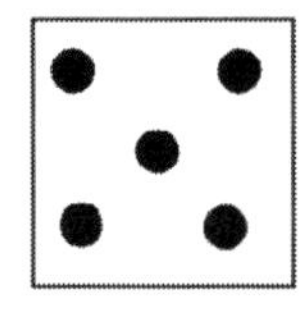 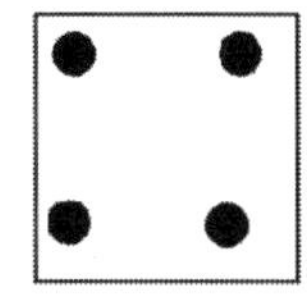 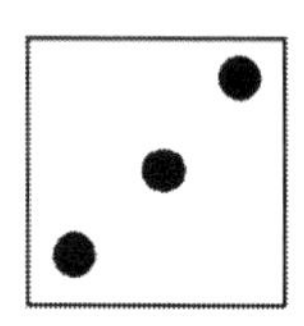

2. Attempting to remember four numbers in a row, with a designated number in front and another number behind, (such as: two – six – four – one with a five in front of the two and a three behind the one).
3. Attempting to remember five numbers in a row, with one number in front and another number behind.

4. Attempting to remember three numbers in a row, but with two other numbers in front, (such as: two – six – four with a five and a three in front of the two).
5. Attempting to remember three numbers in a row, with two numbers in front and one behind.

Continuation Three: Pairs of Numbers

This variation is based on memorising *pairs of numbers.* You start off this phase of the exercise by saying to your child a sequence of three pairs of numbers. Your child should then lay out the dice horizontally, according to the sequence the pairs are presented. Laying out three pairs of dice produces the same result as six single dice and this exercise may not seem to be very different to a straight-line sequence. But for many children, it is more complex. By splitting the sequence into pairs, you are asking your child memorise and then reconstruct the information in a different way.

Explain to your child the principle of laying down pairs of dice and work your way through the variations outlined below.

1. Attempting to remember and reproduce a sequence of three pairs of numbers, (such as: six then two - five then one - four then three).

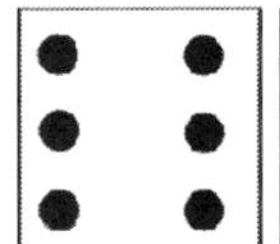 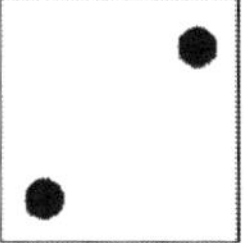 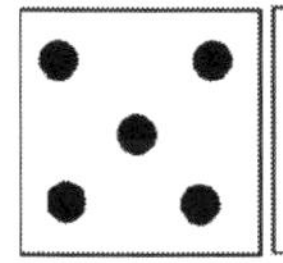  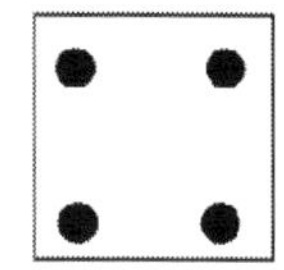 

2. Attempting to remember four and then five pairs of numbers.
3. Vary the task by asking your child to remember pairs of dice based on one number behind another or in front of another, (such as: four behind two - five behind three - six in front of one).

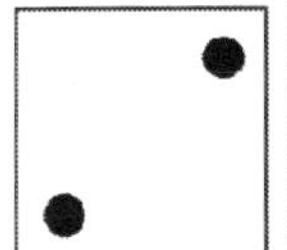 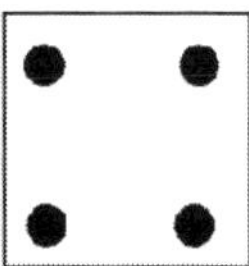 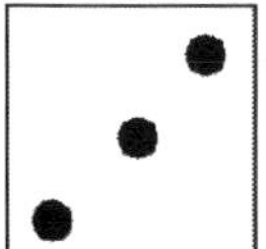 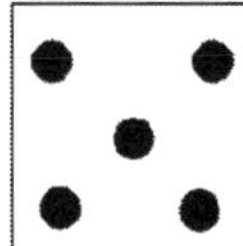 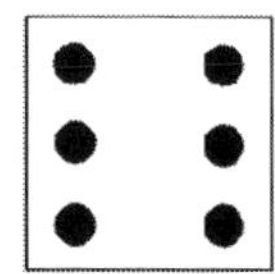 

4. Attempting to remember four and then five pairs of numbers as 3 above.

Continuation Four: See How far You Can Go

With all variations of this exercise, as each step is accomplished you can attempt to push your child a little bit further. For each of the variations, try to increase the number of dice and the complexity of the patterns. Try with five, then six, then seven numbers in a line and with one in front and one behind. Try with more dice above the line and also below the line. See how far you can go and how much you and your child can achieve together but without imposing any pressure to succeed in a certain way or at a particular pace. Each additional number and each extra die on the table, represents an improvement in your child's memory.

Outcome

- Most children, even those with quite severe problems initially, will eventually improve their memory sufficiently to be able to accomplish the first two-dimensional exercise. Many children will be demonstrating a good improvement in their memory retention and sequencing, just by being able to remember a five dice sequence in two dimensions. This should start to be reflected in a more relaxed and effective memory process for everyday matters.
- The exercises are assisting the participant to remember sequences of facts. Memory sequencing capability is a vital part of most academic disciplines, whether it is a sequence of events or of numbers or whatever. This exercise will improve your child's capability to remember facts and then to be able to reproduce the memorized detail in the required sequence.
- The 'in front of/behind/above/below' aspect of the exercise develops improved spatial awareness, which is an important attribute for being able to learn to read and for comprehension of many mathematical concepts.
- The exercise assists children to overcome attention deficit problems; the nature and the intensity of the exercise obliges them to focus only on the task they are trying to accomplish and to shut out of their mind any other distractions.
- This exercise has also been found to bring about improved numeracy, so if you find that your child starts to become better at mathematics, be pleased, but not totally surprised.

Exercise 11/2: Using Coloured Bricks

Introduction

This exercise makes use of children's coloured bricks or cubes for training the memory. These are available from most good toyshops. The child is told an arrangement of bricks and then has to reproduce it with the bricks, from memory. Unlike the previous exercise with the dice, this exercise operates in three dimensions, with the bricks required to be stacked *on top of* each other as well as being placed in front of, or behind, other coloured bricks. You will need a selection of square children's coloured bricks, with at least three bricks of each primary colour.

To Start

The procedure is for children to listen to the spoken instruction, which is a sequence or a pattern of colours and then attempt to reproduce exactly what has been heard, using the coloured bricks.

1. Your child's eyes must be closed while listening.
2. You start the exercise by saying to your child a short sequence of colours, (such as: red - green - blue).
3. You then repeat again the same colour sequence.
4. Now with eyes open, your child has to place the bricks in a straight line, in the sequence that you have said.
5. A colour can be repeated in the sequence, (such as: red – blue – green – blue).

When your child can remember three colours, attempt a four-colour sequence. Most children will be able to accomplish this with some practice. Continue to repeat this exercise for a few minutes about three times a week and until your child can remember the four colour sequence on a consistent basis.

Continuation One: Adding Variations

With this continuation of the exercise, you are asking your child to remember patterns of coloured bricks with some bricks *on top of* the others. This added dimension of *on top*, can represent a major step up in complexity. You may well find that it is too hard for your child and if it cannot be done at all when you first try, then go back to repeating the first part of the exercise and try this new memory task again, a few days later.

For all variations of this exercise, the same principles apply; your child's eyes should be closed when listening to instructions, you say the arrangement of bricks twice, each time slowly and clearly. Now with eyes open, your child has to lay the bricks onto a table to match the pattern you have called out.

Work your way through the variations of arrangement set out below.

1. Attempting to remember a row of four bricks, with an extra brick on top, (such as: red – green – blue – yellow, with a blue on top of the red).
2. Attempting to remember five colours in a row, with another one on top, (such as: red – yellow – green – blue - orange - with a green on top of the blue).
3. Attempting to remember four colours in a row, with two more on top, (such as: blue – green – red – yellow with a blue on top of the green and an orange on top of the red).
4. Attempting to remember five colours in a row, with two more on top.
5. Four colours in a row, with three more on top.
   Continue to practice this exercise, using many different permutations of the colours and arrangements.

Continuation Two: More Complex Patterns in a Row

For this variant of the exercise we move back to using a linear sequence of bricks, without the additional bricks on top. This time a child is asked to remember a sequence of four colours in a row, with another colour to be placed in the line of bricks *in front of and/or behind* the others, all in a horizontal line.

As you progress with the exercise, increase the number of bricks to be remembered. See how far you can go and how much you and your child can achieve together, but without putting any pressure on your child to succeed in a certain way or at a particular pace.

This variant of the exercise should be carried out alongside the previous one; you can alternate them between sessions or you can mix them up in the same session.

Explain to your child the way the bricks are to be put down and what is meant by – 'in front' and 'behind'. Work through the extensions of the exercise outlined below.

1. Attempting to remember and reproduce four colours in a row, with another colour to be placed in front of the row, (such as: red – green – yellow – orange, with a blue to be placed in front of the red).
2. Attempting to remember four colours in a row, with a designated colour in front and another colour behind.
3. Attempting to remember five colours in a row, with one colour in front and another colour behind.
4. Attempting to remember three colours in a row, with two other colours in front, (such as: red - green – yellow, with a blue, then yellow in front of the red).
5. Attempting to remember three colours in a row with two others in front and one behind.

Continuation Three: Pairs of Colours

This exercise now continues with a variation based on memorising pairs of colours. Start off this phase of the exercise by asking your child to remember and set out three pairs of colours in a line, (such as: red then blue- blue then red – green then yellow).

Your child should then place the bricks in a horizontal line, according to the sequence the pairs were presented. Laying out three pairs of bricks produces the same result as six single bricks and this exercise may not seem to be very different to a straight-line sequence. But, by splitting the sequence into pairs, you are asking your child memorise and then reconstruct the information in a different way.

After three pairs can be remembered consistently, progress from there using the variations set out below.

1. Attempting to remember and reproduce, four pairs of colours, (such as: red then blue - green then blue - yellow then orange – red then yellow).
2. Attempting to remember five pairs of colours.
3. For this variation, three pairs of bricks are requested, but in a different way. The exercise is basically the same but the

instructions differ from before. Ask your child to remember and reproduce pairs of bricks in a line, with 'one colour behind' another or 'one colour in front' of another. You might ask your child to place three pairs of bricks in a line: red behind blue - green behind yellow - orange in front of red.

4. Continue to extend both of these variations, increasing the numbers of pairs, as far as your child is able.

Continuation Four: See How far You Can Go

As your child's memory continues to improve, you can make the task more demanding and more interesting, by asking for the bricks to be stacked higher and in more complex permutations.

Mix up bricks *on top* with bricks *in front of or behind*. See how far your child can go and what level of complexity can be remembered.

For example: a row of red – blue – green, with a yellow on top of the blue, an orange on top of the yellow, and a green behind the red.

Outcome

- The use of colour is an effective means of training the auditory memory. This exercise will lead to improvements in a person's capability to remember facts and to be able to reproduce the memorized detail.
- The three dimensional aspect of the exercise helps to resolve weaknesses in spatial awareness, (as explained in chapter seven), which is an important attribute for being able to learn to read and write and for the comprehension of many mathematical concepts.
- The exercise also has been shown to be helpful for people with attention deficit problems (see what Harry has to say about it in chapter four). The necessity to concentrate on and remember the colour patterns can bring about a general improvement in the ability to be able to focus only on the task in hand and shut out any other distractions.

Chapter Twelve

Auditory and Visual Training Exercises

Exercise 12/1: The Encords

Introduction

This chapter contains just one exercise, which is mainly targeted at improving auditory memory. The exercise is based on squares on a grid, with each square identified by the position that it occupies on the grid. Although the primary purpose of the exercise is to train and improve auditory memory, it also requires the child to consider the positioning of the squares and place an object on them and because of this, the exercise also helps children who have visual problems.

As a basis for this exercise, you need to draw a grid as shown below, with the squares across labelled A to E and the squares down the side labelled 1 to 4. The horizontal and vertical co-ordinates identify each square so that square A1 is the top left hand corner and square E4 is the bottom right-hand corner. Use a grid, which is around ten inches wide and eight inches deep, with each individual square being about two inches square.

The operation of the exercise is for the child to remember a number of grid references and place the objects onto the correct square.

You will need a number of small objects to place on the grid, such as draughts, black buttons, small wooden or plastic children's bricks or anything else that is smaller than the size of the individual squares. The contrast of a black draught on the white squares is the ideal combination.

Start the exercise with a grid that has each of the positions labelled, as shown in the first diagram. When your child becomes confident and is able to remember the grid positions most of the time, change to using a grid with just the rows and columns labelled, as shown in the second diagram.

A1	B1	C1	D1	E1
A2	B2	C2	D2	E2
A3	B3	C3	D3	E3
A4	B4	C4	D4	E4

	A	B	C	D	E
1					
2					
3					
4					

With just a little effort you can make it easier for the child who is clumsy, by putting a small piece of Velcro on each square and sticking another piece of Velcro onto the draughts or whatever is used to place on the grid. This will help to prevent the child from knocking the first draught off, when putting the second one in place.

To Start

1. Your child's eyes must be closed while listening.
2. You say to your child three positions on the grid, (such as: A2 - B4 - C3)
3. You can use any of the five alphabetic columns as long as the sequence of grid references is in *alphabetic order.*
4. You repeat again the same co-ordinate number sequence.
5. Your child (with eyes open now) has to remember the positions and place the draughts onto the correct squares, matching those called out.

People with a good memory usually find this simple exercise to be no trouble at all and can easily remember sequences of six and seven positions. But the child with learning difficulties may struggle to remember even three. Plan to start with memorising three positions but be prepared to drop back to two positions, if your child cannot consistently manage to remember three.

The alphabetic left to right sequence will make the memory task easier at first and it is working in the left to right sequence of reading English and other European languages.

You should expect your child to make mistakes at the start, even with only three positions to remember. For many children, this exercise will not be easy, so please do not get impatient if your child fails to remember what may seem to be a very simple sequence.

This is not just an exercise to reproduce what is in short term memory. The sequence of squares needs to be remembered for the duration of the time it takes to locate all of the correct squares and then to place each of the draughts onto the grid. It is only too easy for the position of the final draught to slip away out of memory, before it is put into place. To be accomplished successfully, this exercise usually requires interaction between short term and long-term memory. This will make it challenging for the person for whom this process is not yet fully automatic.

Continuation One: More Squares

When your child can remember three positions consistently then move on to four positions, (such as: A1 - B4 – C3 – E2), still maintaining the alphabetic sequence.

Achievement with this exercise can vary from one day to the next, so if your child is unsuccessful for a while with four positions, then drop the exercise back to remembering three and then at a later time, move forward again to four. It may take some time, possibly weeks or months rather than days, but eventually your child should be able to remember the four positions consistently.

You then continue the memory training with five positions to be remembered, using all of the five alphabetic columns, (such as: A2 – B4 – C1 – D4 - E5), or using one column twice.

Do this exercise for five minutes at first and do not extend it much longer than ten minutes, otherwise it will quickly become tedious. Ask your child to remember no more than five or six sets of positions at each session. Although you need not do this exercise for very long at a time, you should do it regularly, around two or three times a week. The length of the training session is not important; what is more important is the regularity with which the exercise is carried out.

Continuation Two: Mixed Alphabetic Sequence

The second phase of this exercise introduces an apparently simple twist, but it makes the memory task a little more difficult. The change is that the strictly alphabetic sequence is no longer observed and the grid positions are now to be remembered in a sequence that is not alphabetic and is not left to right, (such as: D3 - A1 - E5 - B2).

As before, each time you carry out the exercise, you say the positions to your child and then you repeat them, slowly and clearly. Your child's eyes must be closed while listening to the instructions.

With this change, you will probably find that you need to reduce the number of positions that your child is asked to remember, down from five to two or three. You can then gradually progress back to five positions.

Some children find this extension of the exercise quite difficult and they may never progress far enough, to reach the point where five positions can be remembered. This does not matter. The effort of striving and of attempting to remember will help to improve the child's memory. By contrast, there will be some children who start with a poor memory but who progress to being able to remember seven or eight grid positions or even more.

When moving to this extension of the exercise, you should still continue to carry out the first exercise, which requires memory recall in a left to right sequence.

Continuation Three: A New Sequence

This third phase of the exercise can be done in parallel with phases one and two and should only be started when your child has begun to make good progress with the second variation of the exercise. Another apparently simple change can make the exercise more demanding.

This time, you change the order of the grid reference and start with the numeric element of the grid reference, (such as: 1A - 2C - 4B).

This change can make the square references much more difficult to remember, as the horizontal sequence is broken up and the memory processes are obliged to work in a different way. Once again, start with a two or three square sequence and then gradually work your way up again to as high a number of grid references as can be remembered.

Some people find this variant to be quite difficult. If your child is unable to manage it, then leave it and only use the earlier parts of this exercise.

Timing

If your child makes good enough progress, you may be able to extend the grid, either horizontally beyond five positions or vertically beyond four columns. That applies to all three phases of this exercise.

Whichever part of this exercise you are using, the exercise of remembering co-ordinates should be carried out for a few minutes, two or three times a week, until there is a noticeable improvement. If progress is slow, these exercises can be continued for six months or a year or more. Do not stop these memory exercises, even when there has been a marked improvement in your child's auditory memory. Continue them once a week or perhaps every few weeks for a year or more, to consolidate the changes and continue the improvement in the ability to hear and to remember.

Outcome

- This exercise will improve the auditory memory of the participant.
- The exercise assists in developing and speeding up the mechanisms for transferring information between short term and long term memory.
- The first phase of the exercise is training the memory to view and retain information in a left to right sequence. This will help to strengthen the processes which enable reading to take place and will be reflected in a better ability to remember those English language letter combinations (such as 'ight'), which can present a barrier to fluent reading for children with a weak memory.

Lennie Reads Harry Potter

Lennie came to the Turnabout Programme at the age of twelve, with very many problems. He exhibited severe dyslexic symptoms and also he was heavily dosed with Ritalin to moderate his erratic behaviour.

The background to his situation was that, as a young child, he had suffered from glandular fever, which set him back both physically and educationally. Following his illness, his progress at school was very limited in all subjects, apart from art. He could not read at all and he had a very poor memory for day-to-day activities. But he could copy text and drawings very accurately and with great style.

Like many of the children with the greatest problems, Lennie began his process of turnabout by carrying out the music-based exercises, which helped him with his concentration. Following that, he was given intensive training to improve his auditory and visual memory.

Lennie needed to work hard at all of the exercises he was given and he did. He made good progress in all areas and his hyperactivity gradually began to subside. Towards the end of his first year of Turnabout training there was a major breakthrough. Lennie began to read! By the end of this single year of training, Lennie was able to read a complete book for himself for the first time. In his excitement, Lennie showed everyone that he could keep up with the fashion as well as the next man. The very first book he read all the way through was `Harry Potter and the Philosopher's Stone'.

Chapter Thirteen

Exercises to Develop Visual Memory

The exercises in the previous three chapters have mainly concentrated on aspects of the auditory capabilities. We now focus upon ways of developing the visual processes. In this chapter, we introduce three important exercises for improving the processing of visual stimuli and enhancing the workings of the visual memory. These exercises are likely to benefit most children with severe or moderate learning difficulties and we recommend that they should not be missed out for any dyslexic child.

Exercise 13/1: Matching Up Geometric Shapes

Purpose

This is a 'starter' exercise that begins the process of redressing weaknesses in a child's visual capabilities.

To Start

This exercise is based on visualising and then matching up, geometric shapes. You will need some coloured wooden or plastic flat geometric shapes, which can be bought from toyshops or educational supply shops. A box of mixed children's bricks can also be used for this purpose. The shapes need to be a selection of the common ones; such as squares, rectangles, triangles, circles and semi-circles. You need about four or five examples of each shape, with a range of primary colours and with at least two of each shape/colour; such as two red circles, two red triangles, two red squares, two red rectangles, two red semi-circles, two green circles etc.

You carry out this simple exercise as follows:

1. Show your child one of the shapes, such as a semi-circle

2. Ask your child to pick out all of the pieces on the table that are the same shape, irrespective of colour.
3. Your child then lays out all of the pieces of the same shape together onto a table or onto any flat surface.

For the younger child, you can turn it a more lively game, by sticking magnetic tape onto the back of the shapes and then using them as a fridge magnets or placing them onto a metal backing sheet (such as a baking tin). Alternatively, and again for younger children, you could ask them to stick all of the pieces of the chosen shape onto a sheet of paper or onto card with paste. This has the added benefit of introducing some learning through touch, as well as through sight.

Continuation

This exercise might appear to be overly simplistic, but many dyslexic children have a problem distinguishing one shape from another and very often, they do not find this apparently simple task to be at all easy at first. But whatever the early difficulties, this activity needs to be sustained and continued on a regular basis. If your child struggles initially and is unable to do it, then leave it for a week or so and then try again. For other children, this exercise will appear very simple and if that is the case with your own child, then move straight on to the next exercise. The following exercise also uses geometric shapes but in a more demanding way. However long it takes to master, continue with this first exercise until your child can do it quite easily, before you move on to the next one.

Outcome

With practise, the exercise will help children with weak visual capabilities. It will begin the improvement in spatial awareness and it will train the eye to differentiate one shape from another.

Exercise 13/2: Multiple Shapes for Memory Training

Purpose

This is a very effective exercise for training visual memory. The exercise continues the use of the shapes, but this time they are to be shown to your child and memorised. As before, the shapes should include squares, rectangles, circles, semi-circles, triangles and diamonds, in a mix of colours. Begin the exercise with one colour only.

To Start

1. Lay out onto a flat surface, a pattern of shapes that your child will have to memorise and then recreate.
2. Start off with three pieces, all laid out in a horizontal line, (such as: a red circle, a red triangle and a red square).
3. Allow your child time to view and memorise the shapes and their arrangement. Allow a time equivalent to about two seconds per shape.
4. Cover up the shapes and ask your child to recreate that pattern, with other equivalent shapes.

Keep things simple and easy when you start. You can then move on to asking your child to remember slightly more complex arrangements, (such as: two circles in a horizontal line with a triangle underneath one of the circles).

As you progress and your child is able to remember and recreate simple patterns, you gradually make the mix of shapes and patterns more complex and more demanding.

Memorising shapes in this way is hard for the child who has visual memory problems. Therefore, start off this exercise using one colour only and gradually increase the number of shapes to be remembered, from three to four and then to five. There are, of course, many possible arrangements of the geometric shapes.

Continuation: Mixing the colours

When your child can comfortably remember four or five shapes of one colour, you are ready to introduce a *mix of colours*. At this stage, you may need to go back to only using three shapes.

1. Lay out a pattern of shapes that your child is to memorise and then recreate.
2. Start off with three pieces of different colours, all put down in a horizontal line, (such as: a red circle, a blue triangle and a green square).
3. Allow your child time to view and to memorise the shapes and their arrangement. Allow a time equivalent to about two seconds per shape.
4. Cover up the shapes and ask your child to recreate that pattern with other equivalent shapes, laying them flat onto the table. This time there must be a colour match.

As you continue with the exercise, your child should be required to view, retain and recreate many different combinations of shapes and colours. You can gradually increase the number of shapes to be remembered, (such as: a blue square, a red circle, a green triangle in a horizontal line with a yellow square above the circle or a red semi-circle underneath the blue square).

The basic shapes can be rotated so that, for instance, the semi-circles can have the circular shape at the top or bottom, triangles can point up, down or sideways. Each of these variants helps to extend and to strengthen the visual memory.

Each step up in the number of shapes used or the complexity of the patterns, may need a considerable period of time (possibly some weeks), before it is mastered. Even allowing for this, you should be able to progress so that your child can remember four and then five shapes and then with time, be able to recall six and seven different shapes and colours. Some children, who started with a very weak visual memory, have been able to memorise and reproduce patterns of up to ten shapes. This should not be seen as a target but if your child struggles at first, you should both know that it will get easier with time.

Outcome

By using this exercise with a multiplicity of shapes and colours, we are training the child to do a number of things:

- To be able to visualise accurately,
- To absorb the visual information into memory,
- To organise the information effectively and then to subsequently retrieve and display the information that has been memorised.

Each of these skills is a vital component of the learning process and any or all of them may have been lacking in the child classified as dyslexic.

Exercise 13/3. Using Dice For Memory Training

Purpose

This is an exercise, primarily for improving visual memory. It makes use of dice, in a similar way to their use in the auditory exercise in chapter eleven. Within this exercise, the child is required to observe and then to recreate an arrangement of the dice.

To Start

This exercise needs a quantity of six dice, which should be conventional six sided dice. For this exercise, the colour of the dice is greatly significant and the dice should be either white dice with black spots or black dice with white spots. Either is suitable but the colours must be black and white, which have particular characteristics for improving visual memory. Generally, the larger the dice, the easier they are to use and the sets of dice available from toy shops are sometimes a little larger than those that come out of children's games.

The exercise is very straightforward and works as follows:

1. You draw on to paper a picture of three dice, in a horizontal or vertical line. You can draw the picture at the time you carry out the exercise or it can be prepared before you start. You show the picture to your child
2. You allow your child some time to view and memorise the picture of the dice; a total time equivalent to approximately five seconds per die, is about right.
3. You then cover up the picture.

4. The task for your child is to memorise the pattern of the dice in the picture and then to recreate it from memory, using some or all of the dice.

Start the exercise with a simple pattern using three dice only or two dice if your child cannot manage to remember three. As soon as your child is able to memorise and recreate this simple layout, you should move on to using four dice, also in simple arrangements, either in vertical, horizontal or diagonal lines. Some children will be able to proceed very quickly from two to three to four dice but for others, it may take some weeks, before they can make these steps.

Continuation

The next step is to draw an arrangement with the dice that has several dice laid flat in a horizontal row, with another die laid flat below the line, (such as: a four, a two, a five and a one in a horizontal line, with a six below the five). Once again your child needs to view this arrangement and then recreate it from memory.

Vary the patterns of the dice, sometimes to have numbers above and sometimes below, a horizontal line. Alternatively, arrange the dice in a vertical line with one or two other dice alongside. When these types of pattern can be remembered, then move up to five and then six dice. Ten will probably be as high as you need to reach but if your child makes very good progress, you can use one or two more. However many dice you use and whatever the pattern, your child should be given a period of time, equivalent to around five seconds per die, to study the picture and attempt to remember the pattern of the dice.

Outcome

- This simple exercise will strengthen a weak visual memory. There is the additional benefit of needing to visualise and remember the numbers on the dice, which in itself is helpful to children with low numeracy skills.
- All of the three exercises in this chapter address weaknesses in aspects of visual processing; they improve the accuracy with which images and written information are perceived, understood and

remembered. These exercises also help to speed up the memory processes; speed is vital for effective functioning of the memory.

Alex: Intelligent - But Cannot Read and Comprehend

At the age of fourteen, Alex had been excluded from school following a history of truancy, lateness, lies and considerable disruption.

Alex was an extremely intelligent young man, but full of frustration. He could understand the explanations in class much quicker than anyone else and he was then impatient with the rest of the class and very disruptive. But notwithstanding his intelligence and his ability to quickly comprehend quite complex matters, Alex could not read fluently nor could he understand the meaning of the words as he read them.

Interestingly, Alex came from a multilingual background but unusually, there was no dominant language and Alex did not appear to have a natural mother tongue.

When he started the Turnabout Programme, Alex demonstrated a great contrast. He could handle the auditory exercises with ease, but he had great problems with all of the visually based activities. Alex was given training that would enhance his visual processing and he worked at the visual memory exercises. All of his work was in one language, which became predominant. During the next year, the training began to take effect and Alex started to read and to understand the words he read. His behavioural problems that had come about as a cover for his comprehension difficulties were left behind.

Alex was allowed back into school and at the age of sixteen, he moved on to high school. He still finds it difficult to work with others and he remains impatient with people who are not as quick on the uptake as himself, including one or two of his teachers. Alex seems to be destined for university and an academic life; his work is of a high standard particularly with major projects and he is at his happiest working alone on project based activities.

Perhaps a little reluctant to admit to himself that he ever had problems, Alex is typical of many dyslexic people; very intelligent, very capable in some areas but extremely weak in others. If we can help them to overcome their weaknesses, then people like Alex can go on to fulfil their great potential.

Chapter Fourteen

Exercises for Enhanced Visual Processing

Some of the exercises in this chapter are variations on traditional games and pastimes and they may seem familiar. Nevertheless, they are all worthwhile activities and each will help to develop the underlying skills necessary for effective reading and writing. We are using them here, in a measured repetitive way, to build up the visual strengths that are likely to be lacking in a dyslexic person. Most of these exercises can be treated as games that both you and your child should be able to enjoy carrying out. For the younger child, the first three exercises are designed to link together, with each one having to be accomplished before moving on to the next. We sometimes bypass the first two exercises for an older child.

Exercise 14/1: Memorising missing objects

Introduction

This exercise requires the child to view and memorise objects. It can be carried out occasionally for a few minutes; perhaps at meal times or in spare moments.

To Start

1. You need to place four objects on a table, preferably with all four objects having something in common. For example you might use objects related to writing, (such as: a pen, an eraser, a pencil and a sharpener). Or you could use items of crockery (such as: a saucer, a plate, a cup, and a mug,) or any other set of four familiar items.
2. Ask your child to look at the objects for a total time equivalent to about two seconds per object. During this time, your child has

to attempt to memorise all of the objects. Extend the time if you believe that your child needs to view the objects for a little longer.

3. With your child's eyes closed or with your child looking away, you remove *one* of the objects.
4. With your child's eyes now open, you ask the question: Which one has gone?

Continuation

If the exercise is too easy with four objects, continue at a level that your child will find more difficult, but not impossible. Increase the number of objects to five then six or more, but still removing one object only. Many children starting with very poor memories have struggled at first, but after carrying out the exercise for some time, they have improved to such an extent that they have been able to identify the one missing item from as many as ten other objects. Exceptionally, some children have been able to pick one missing item from twenty objects.

Outcome

This simple exercise will improve the visual memory and enhance spatial awareness. In practical terms, it will help to overcome those weaknesses that may have prevented accurate spelling.

Exercise 14/2: Memorising the sequence of objects

Introduction

This exercise is an effective means of training the memory to recall information in the sequence that it is needed. It should be used on an occasional basis, alongside the other visual training exercises. The exercise is based on remembering the sequence into which a range of objects has been placed.

To Start

1. Start the exercise with four familiar objects, all of which have something in common (such as a plate, a saucer, a cup and a mug). Place them in a row on the table.

2. Your child needs to study these objects for a time equivalent to about two seconds per object.
3. Either with your child's eyes closed or with your child looking away, you shuffle the objects around into a different sequence.
4. The task for your child is to replace the objects back in their original positions.

Continuation

When your child can re-sequence four objects accurately, then you can progress to using five objects, then six and however many more can be managed. Try to vary the content in order to keep the interest alive. Use a wide range of objects to view and memorise; such as photographs, crockery, pictures of celebrities or footballers, sporting paraphernalia or whatever. Preferably, they should be items that your child is interested in, but they do not have to be.

Outcome

The exercise encourages information to be retrieved in the required sequence. It will underpin improved spelling capability and can help children to recognize and remember common words.

Exercise 14/3: Drawing the missing picture

Introduction

This is a memory training exercise that should be undertaken when the previous exercise can be completed fairly easily. Success with this exercise will indicate that there has been a good improvement in the visual processes and in visual memory. Do not be discouraged by the apparent difficulty. Many dyslexic children, who have reached this stage, have managed it well.

To Start

1. You need to place a number of pictures on a table. For the younger child, start off with just two pictures and as your child becomes more proficient, you can build up the number. Use more pictures for the older child. Try to find pictures that your child can relate

to or that have a common theme. The pictures can be whatever you have around the house; newspaper photos, holiday snapshots, pictures of animals, fashion pictures from magazines; use what you have available and is appropriate for the age of the child.

2. Ask your child to review and memorise the pictures. There is no need to set a time limit for viewing the pictures. The time needed will depend on the complexity of the pictures, but twenty to thirty seconds in total, is usually sufficient.
3. With your child's eyes closed, you remove one of the pictures.
4. The task for your child is to *attempt to draw* the picture that has been removed.
5. It does not matter at all whether or not your child can draw well. The objective of this training is to encourage the ability to visualise the relationship of all of the main features of the picture to each other.

Continuation

After your child can manage the exercise with two pictures, you need to gradually increase the number of pictures, the complexity of the pictures and the range of subjects. With each progression, the memory is extended by having to remember details of all of the pictures and then reproduce only one picture. As the number of pictures is increased, allow a little more time for your child to visualize and remember them.

Outcome

This exercise develops the capability to focus on and discern details, to visualise shapes and their relationship with each other, to memorise visual images and to recall and represent what has been memorised. Practice with this exercise will, in due course, enable better word recognition when reading and spelling and will assist a person to deal with maps and with diagrams.

Letters That Fly: The Story Of Celine

When fifteen-year-old Celine was referred to the Turnabout Programme, it was for an attention deficit problem but in reality she had a condition known as 'Magnocellular Hypothesis Visual Deficiency'. With this condition, when a person is reading, the letters break up, appear to turn to 'flies', and move across the page. Celine had experienced this strange and unnerving phenomenon ever since she started to learn to read.

When, after some early tests, this was diagnosed, Celine was absolutely amazed that anyone could possibly have suspected it. She had never spoken about it, either at home or at school, for fear that people would think that she was unstable. This had, of course, made school very difficult for Celine and had turned her into a nervous and unhappy person. This unusual condition presented a particular challenge to the Turnabout Programme. Which of the exercises should Celine be encouraged to carry out and how would they work for her difficult problem?

Celine started with the musical exercises (she proved to have an extraordinarily good musical 'ear') but mainly she worked with the visual memory exercises based on remembering articles, as described in this chapter, and also the multiple-shapes memory exercises explained in the previous chapter. With the help of these exercises, she found that she was gradually becoming able to control her condition. Before Celine started the training, the letters 'flew' every single time that she tried to read, but as she progressed she began to see the shapes of the letters properly. As she continued with the memory exercises, the letters remained rooted to the page more and more frequently and for longer periods, and also the length of time between each occurrence of the symptoms began to increase. After six months on the Turnabout Programme, Celine was in control. She had learned to close her eyes when the 'flies' started affecting her reading, and when she did so, they ceased and she could continue to read normally.

Now Celine reads a great deal and finds the letters flying much less frequently but when they do, she now knows how to react and manage the situation. As her symptoms became less frequent so did her apparent attention deficit. Celine is now achieving very high marks in all subjects.

Exercise 14/4: Using the Calendar for Memory Training

Introduction

All too often, the problems that dyslexic children can have with memory, will manifest themselves as an inability to deal with important everyday concepts, such as being unable to recall with any confidence, the days of the week or the months of the year. For children over the age of seven, this can be a major source of embarrassment, as it gives a public face to the problems that they may have tried hard to conceal.

This exercise can be used as a game, to be played occasionally. The objective is to enhance the ability to remember and recall information in the desired sequence. It has the additional benefit of strengthening knowledge of the calendar.

To Start

The whole process is very simple. You ask straightforward questions that oblige children to think about the sequence of the days in the week or months of the year. In order to answer the question, they will have to recall the day or month sequence and this will assist with the process of fixing the whole calendar process more solidly into memory. For this exercise, suitable questions might be

- ☑ What is the third day of the week?
- ☑ What is the fifth month of the year?
- ☑ What is the month before August?
  and other similar questions.

Children with a long history of learning difficulties will probably need to have a very simple calendar on hand, to look at and to help them answer the questions. Even with a printed calendar, the exercise is useful mental training. The child is obliged to look at the sequence of days or months, to practice reading the days and months, and to learn how to make use of a calendar, all of which are valuable skills.

For questions based on days, the calendar will need to show all of the days of the week on one page. For questions based on months, the calendar should show all of the months sequentially on one page. If you do not have such a calendar available, then you can write all of the days and months on a chart, from top to bottom.

A younger child is sometimes able to learn the months more easily if you draw or stick onto the calendar, a picture that represents the month, next to the name of the month. For example, show rain next to April, a sun next to July etc. In this way the child is helped, by learning through 'association'.

Continuation

Continue this exercise with the calendar to hand until you sense that a little confidence is beginning to emerge, and then you can start to ask the occasional question without use of the written calendar. Most children will eventually reach a state in which the exercise is carried out wholly by memory and without a printed calendar as support.

Outcome

This exercise provides both auditory and visual training, which serves to train and strengthen a child's memory. It also provides the additional benefits of teaching and consolidating the essential knowledge of the calendar and helping to eliminate any embarrassment brought about by a weakness in this area. When children have struggled previously, it is by no means a small matter for them to become secure in their knowledge and use of days and months.

Knowing The Calendar: The Story of James

Many participants in the Turnabout Programme were found to have high academic potential, which has subsequently been fulfilled. But not everyone has such ambitions or abilities. For some seriously dyslexic children, just being able to read and write normally will have a major impact upon their lives; their prospects for worthwhile employment, their level of self-esteem and their ability to enjoy life.

James came to the Turnabout Programme at the age of fifteen, with one of the most severe cases of dyslexia that the programme has ever confronted. He had suffered from major learning difficulties all of his life. As a very young child, he did not develop language as quickly as his brothers and sisters. Shortly after starting school, he was placed in a special needs group and following that, he remained within this and similar groups throughout his school career. James had been given counselling, occupational therapy, and assessments by child psychologists, none of which helped him to function at school.

When he started his training, James had a full range of educational and personal problems which included; severe dyslexia with his reading hampered by low word recognition; hyperactivity, only partially controlled by very high dosages of Ritalin; major problems in attention and concentration; poor speaking skills; minimal writing capability and almost no comprehension of mathematics.

James had just one attribute in his favour but it was an important one. He was prepared to work hard. It was apparent that James needed help to develop his concentration and that both his verbal and his written memory were very poor. As expected, progress was very slow, and it was extremely hard going for him and also for the people helping him. There is no magic wand that can put right so many problems in an instant. But with effort and determination, progress can be made, even for a person with such severe learning difficulties.

Among the memory training activities that James carried out, was the exercise in this chapter that utilises the calendar. He developed his own written calendar to help him organize and sequence his day and his week and then eventually his month. He became gradually more organized (albeit with a few lapses). For James, the fact that he was able to manage his own time was a turning point. A major source of embarrassment had now been eliminated and he felt able to tackle all of the other exercises with renewed vigour and optimism.

After one year of hard work, the once very severely dyslexic James can now read properly and fluently, even if a little slowly and he can function in the mainstream of school life, outside of the remedial groups. He will still need help and coaching with his education for some time, but the important thing is that he will leave school and will go out into the world with the tools to cope with life. James's parents, who have suffered many years of disappointment, frustration and despair, are now quite emotional and overwhelmingly appreciative.

Exercise 14/5: Using the alphabet for memory training

Introduction

This is an exercise, suitable for the younger child, that makes use of the letters of the alphabet training the memory. It can be done when you have a few minutes of spare time. This does not replace the work of the school, nor are we seeking to directly teach children the alphabet. However, many dyslexic children and other children with a learning problem, find it difficult to remember the letters of the alphabet and their sequence. (Although, if a child cannot recite the alphabet in sequence, that is not necessarily a barrier to literacy.)

If you do not already have one, you will need to set up a frieze, with all of the letters of the alphabet from A to Z laid out in a series of horizontal lines. The upper and lower case letters should be shown together, e.g. Aa Bb and so on. This is a simple visual aid, which can be purchased from many toyshops or you can draw it up yourself. You can pin it up on the wall in your child's room or lay it out on a table for the purpose of carrying out the exercise.

If your child's recollection of the alphabet is initially very weak, as it is for many dyslexic children, then you can start by breaking the alphabet down into sub-sets of five, six or seven consecutive letters, depending on the severity of difficulty. For instance, you might draw out the first few letters as shown below.

Aa Bb Cc Dd Ee Ff Gg

To Start

Ask your child questions based on this restricted sub-set of the alphabet, such as:

- ☑ What is the third letter of the alphabet?
- ☑ What letter comes before F?
- ☑ How many letters after C is G?

These questions can be answered at first, with the child viewing the frieze to work out the answers. You can then progress to have your child answering the questions fully or partially from memory. When you have done this a few times with the first subset of letters, then do it with the next six or so letters, until you have worked through the whole alphabet.

Continuation

When your child is familiar with most of the letters of the alphabet, you can then ask questions based on the whole alphabet such as:

- ☑ What is the fourth letter of the alphabet?
- ☑ What is the eighth letter?

- ☑ What the letter comes before G?
- ☑ How many letters from the end is W?

Outcome

Occasional use of this exercise can assist in improving your child's auditory and visual memory. Additional benefits that this brings about, in helping to consolidate the knowledge of the letters of the alphabet, will have very direct and obvious advantages for the process of learning to read.

Exercise 14/6: Making Jigsaw Puzzles Work For You

Introduction

It may surprise some people to find that putting together jigsaw puzzles is one of the most effective ways of improving a child's visual capability. Jigsaw puzzles are greatly beneficial; they develop competence in figure/ground discrimination and they enhance spatial awareness. When attempting even the simplest jigsaw puzzle, a child is obliged to focus on the whole picture, while still needing to see the individual shapes which are an element of a whole. Jigsaw puzzles are also effective as a training medium because they are multi-sensory, in that they use the visual senses and also involve learning by the sense of touch.

To Start

For the child who has never undertaken a jigsaw puzzle before, or who has previously tried and been unsuccessful, you will need to start with something quite simple, before moving on to larger and more complex puzzles. And with such children, it may take some effort to persuade them to make a start. When selecting jigsaw puzzles, try to find those that have a strongly differentiated foreground and background. Start at a very basic level, so that your child is able to complete all of the puzzle or a reasonable part of it. It may take several sessions before your child can complete the first puzzle. From then on, continue with relatively easy puzzles and gradually increase the number of pieces and the complexity of the picture. Some children, when starting back with jigsaw puzzles after a gap of a few years, find that they can do them with ease. If your own child fits into this category, you can increase the complexity of the puzzles quite quickly.

The location is important. A child must have a few minutes of peace and quiet away from the family and the television. For a child with siblings, you may need to insist that the jigsaw has to be completed without their assistance.

Sometimes, it is better that the puzzle be done at first with the help of a parent and after that, by encouraging the child to complete it without assistance. You can help out with an occasional piece and if necessary, you should assist your child to organise the pieces so that, for instance, the corner pieces are put into place, the outside pieces are sorted out together, the pieces of the same part of the jigsaw such as water, castle, sky etc are sorted together. Although these strategies may be natural to the person that has done puzzles over the years, they may need to be explained to a new 'jigsaw puzzler'. Some children will want to repeat the same puzzle, again and again, and this is fine.

Continuation

Gradually introduce more difficult and larger puzzles. Also, when a simple jigsaw has been completed, turn over the pieces so that only the blank backs are visible. Then ask your child to have a try at doing the puzzle without the benefit of the picture, fitting the pieces together only using their shapes. If your child can manage to do all or part of the puzzle in this way, it is good training for the visual processes. Some children will be able to do this and some will not.

A few decades ago, before television was commonplace, families would often sit together for hours to complete a jigsaw puzzle. Building a large puzzle is an activity that the whole family can be involved with, and in this way, the child with learning difficulties can be part of the game, without being embarrassed by others being a bit quicker. As part of a family activity, the dyslexic child can be given a special task, such as looking for corners or side-pieces, or finding and fitting pieces of sand or sky or whatever. The family-based approach is particularly helpful in attempting to train teenagers, for whom the picture and the nature of many of the simpler puzzles available can appear too juvenile for their emotional development. In a family environment, a child can gain the benefit of visualising shapes against the background, without any pressure and indeed, without it being apparent that it is a training exercise.

Outcome

Jigsaw puzzles are a game, free from the tensions of the classroom. They are very good for training a child who has weaknesses in aspects of visual competence and they improve a child's ability to concentrate on a single task without distraction.

Jigsaw Puzzles Start the Turnabout: The Story Of Simon

Simon is the third son of academic parents, who had great ambitions for their children to match their own success at school and university. Their eldest two sons have more than met these high expectations, but Simon was very much slower to pick things up, even though his mother, a teacher, gave him considerable help. Simon's parents could not come to terms with the fact that they had a child who could not read or write properly and they found it difficult to face up to the fact that Simon was dyslexic. His problems were already apparent at elementary school but his parents refused to acknowledge them and would not let him be put into a 'special needs' category.

When he went to secondary school, Simon was categorised as having severe learning difficulties and he was promptly placed into a remedial group. His parents, shocked and upset, at last recognised that there was a problem and Simon was referred for an assessment. Carol Goldfus was surprised to meet a child who was nervous and unwilling to speak, and who erased all of his writing as soon as he had written it, as if he was frightened of the consequences.

Simon began the exercises within the Turnabout Programme and he particularly enjoyed the musical activities. Simon also worked hard at the various memory exercises. The low level at which Simon started the exercises, illustrated just how short and ineffective was his working memory. This deficiency alone would have accounted for most of his problems with reading. In the years before he started the Turnabout Programme, Simon's whole education had been impacted by his weak memory and poor spatial awareness. As a result, he could not place letters in the correct position in the word, he could not grasp the sequence of letters when he was reading, nor could he place them in the right order when writing.

The Turning Point!

At first, Simon's progress was quite slow, but the breakthrough came when he began doing jigsaw puzzles for the very first time in his life. Simon found that he could complete a 40-piece puzzle fairly easily and then he started completing puzzles at home on a regular basis. (At the very least this took him away from spending his time with his games machine and watching television.) Simon progressed very quickly and soon was able to complete a 2000 piece jigsaw. As well as enhancing his visual awareness, jigsaw puzzles helped Simon impose a degree of structure and autonomy in his life; the puzzles were something under his own control. Both Simon and his parents were thrilled and they showed everybody what he had accomplished.

The memory training exercises were crucial, but alongside these, his enthusiasm for jigsaw puzzles gave Simon hours of practice of developing the ability to concentrate and increase his spatial intelligence skills.

Throughout his time at school, Simon had become accustomed to many concessions being made to accommodate his learning difficulties, including receiving additional time for class work and being allowed to erase his writing many times. The Turnabout training does not encourage concessions of this type and from the beginning, Simon was not allowed to erase. He was told that he must move forward and not look back. Eventually Simon lost his fear of making mistakes and he become much more self-reliant.

After only one year on the programme, Simon started to see quite dramatic improvements in his results at school. Shortly after that, he was moved out of the remedial group and in mathematics, he was placed into the second stream out of four. Simon bypassed the lowest stream in all subjects, and he was able to cope well with the work in the higher streams.

Simon is no longer the nervous and timid individual of the previous year, but is lively and self-confident. The achievement of actually being able to complete a jigsaw puzzle began to bring about this enhanced self-image and started him on the process of `turnabout`.

Summary

The exercises in this chapter and the previous one, will bring about a substantial improvement in the memory of the participant. This will be translated into a greatly improved capability in many practical areas.

Most of the exercises lend themselves to measuring and recording progress over a period of time. If you do this, then when you look back over several months, you may be astonished by the improvement. As you move forward with the exercises, review the progress and the remarkable achievements that have been brought about by the hard work of your child and yourself, and *celebrate!*

Section 4

Managing The Turnabout

Chapter Fifteen

Is There a Hearing Problem?

This chapter has one primary message. There have been cases where a child has had a hearing problem that has persisted for many years, unsuspected by the parents and this has proved to be the sole cause of the child's educational difficulties. Therefore, we ask you to consider whether or not your child might have a physical hearing difficulty and if you are at all concerned, you should see a doctor.

Before proceeding with the exercises to improve auditory capabilities, try to make a judgement. How well does my child hear? Is there any possibility at all of there being a physical hearing deficiency? Within this chapter we have some simple tests that you can apply, if you are unsure about the matter. But these should not detract from the main message. If you have any doubts at all, seek medical assistance.

The Younger Child

Physical hearing problems are quite common in nursery age and young school children, who may have 'glue ear' or have their ears partially blocked through the after-affects of colds or infections. Poor hearing capability will affect your child's learning and behaviour, until it is rectified.

With the younger child, you may start to suspect that there could be a hearing problem, when your child does not respond when called; that is constantly, as opposed to normal childhood awkwardness or assertiveness. This failure to respond to you may indicate that a hearing problem exists. Also, some children display a blank or tense face when apparently listening or there can a tilting of the head when spoken to; these are indicators of a possible medical problem.

The Reluctant Teenager

The very simple hearing tests that follow are suited to younger children, but even the thought of being tested in this way may provoke an unhelpful response from a teenager. If you cannot easily persuade your teenage child to co-operate, you may need to look for more generalised indicators and clues that suggest that there may be a problem.

An indication that something may be amiss with your child's hearing, can be the extreme sound from an overloud television, radio or stereo. A high volume of sound is, of course, not an unusual characteristic of musical appreciation, for any teenager. You can assess whether this represents a potential medical problem, by judging whether or not your child's head is consistently closer than you might expect to the loudspeaker. If your child is physically very close to the source of the sound and perhaps with the head inclined to the side, this may be an indication of a physical hearing problem. Exceptional closeness to a very loud television can also give you an indication that there may be a possible physical hearing disability.

If you are quite certain that your own child has no physical hearing problem, then, of course, you should proceed to carry out the Turnabout exercises in section three. But, if you suspect that there might be a hearing problem, then you need to resolve this issue one way or another. You may decide to go straight to your doctor and that is what we recommend. However, we have set out below, three simple tests, which you can apply before deciding to seek medical help. They are not definitive and should only be used as a guide. If, as a result of these tests, physical hearing problems are suspected, then you should seek medical advice immediately, so that the physical impediment can be investigated and hopefully corrected.

The Hearing Tests

Here are some very simple tests that can help you assess whether your child might have is a hearing problem

The whisper test

For this test, you should sit behind your child, at a distance of around three or four metres. You then give directions to your child in a whisper or low tone of voice but at a level you would expect to be heard. These can be quite simple directives such as, "stand up", "lift up your arms", "move your head to the left" and other similar instructions. Watch your child carefully. Usually, children who cannot hear correctly will move in a gradual way to shorten the distance between you and them. This, as with the following tests, is not an infallible guide but is an indicator that you should have your child's hearing checked out medically.

Differentiating sounds

For this test, you use children's toys to make very distinct sounds, such as ringing a bell and beating a drum and then you ask your child to identify the sound that was made. From this test, it is at once apparent whether or not there is a hearing problem. This test should be carried out with your child's eyes shut.

The ticking watch test

If you still have a watch or clock that ticks or if you can borrow one, then screen your child's head with a card so that the watch cannot be seen. Place the child's finger over one ear and hold the watch close to the other ear. Ask your child to tell you when the ticking can be heard. If there is very little response to the ticking, you are alerted to a possible problem that might need medical attention. It is possible that only one ear will not react properly to the ticking watch test, in which it will still need further medical investigation.

If your child cannot do any of these tests with certainty, then it is appropriate to ask for medical assistance. If there is a physiological problem, then this is most likely to be the main cause of the learning difficulties that have been encountered so far, and there is no point in attempting any of the remedial exercises in this book, until it is resolved.

The main message of this chapter is important and it is worth repeating. If you have any doubts or concerns about your child's hearing, consult a doctor.

Chapter Sixteen

The Parent As Trainer

By undertaking the Turnabout Programme, you will have both the pleasure and responsibility of helping your own child. In order to make the task more readily achievable by parents who, although caring and committed, are not teachers, we have set out some advice on how to go about the training process

The emphasis throughout must be on patience, as you will be attempting to correct a range of conditions that may have taken root over many years. We can guide and advise you, but no one knows your children better than you and all children are different. It is for you to use your judgement in managing the programme; deciding how long to continue a particular exercise, when to praise and when to be firm.

Relating to The School

It is most likely that the school your child attends will be giving traditional reading exercises. This is almost certainly so within the primary school environment and may well be the case, if your child is receiving remedial help in a secondary school. The Turnabout Programme does not incorporate these traditional reading practices. We emphasise that there is no conflict with the work of the schools. The Turnabout exercises will develop a child's ability to cope with traditional schoolwork, through creating better pathways and processes in the brain. Whether or not you tell the school that you are undertaking this programme will be up to you. Some teachers will not have heard of these exercises or this particular approach; some will be very supportive, others may be sceptical and you need to be prepared for this. You may also chose to say nothing and wait until the day when the school informs you that, quite suddenly, your child has made a breakthrough and that reading and writing are much improved.

Planning the Programme

The descriptions of the exercises in the book include guidance on how frequently they should be carried out and for how long. There are some 'core' exercises that have greater impact than others and therefore should be done regularly and repetitively. There are also exercises described as 'occasional'. Although these are an important part of the programme, they can be done on a less regular basis.

Even for the professional educator, it can sometimes be difficult to diagnose which of the exercises should be selected to match the symptoms of any particular child, so we should not expect it to be easy for the layperson. Try all of the core exercises at first. If your child finds any exercise to be particularly easy, this will indicate that there is probably not a problem with the particular area of learning that the exercise addresses. Many dyslexic children have a 'spiky' profile; being very capable in some areas and poor in others, and you should give greater time and higher priority to the exercises that strengthen the weaker areas. It can still be beneficial to intersperse these with some of the exercises that your child finds easier, so that each session is not a continuous struggle.

Managing The Training

Any individual child will take to some exercises more readily than to others. Initially, if your own child is more comfortable with certain exercises and shows strong resistance to others, then carry on with those exercises that have been well accepted and leave until a later time, any which generate an adverse reaction. But, notwithstanding any initial resistance, you should return later to these exercises, as they may be the ones that will be most beneficial in the long run. Sometimes, if children rebel against a specific exercise, it is because they are trying too hard and attempting to advance too fast for their capabilities. If you find that you are completely stalled with one particular exercise, leave it and return to it after a gap of a week or two.

Most of the exercises are progressive in nature. All of them have a low starting point, which is set so that most dyslexic children will have the encouragement of some early success. But even this low level can be difficult for some children. You will need to establish, fairly quickly, whether or not your child finds the starting level to be easy or difficult.

If the exercise is found to be too easy, then extend the scope until you are starting at a level that your child can accomplish, but only with some difficulty. If your child starts to find an exercise to be too difficult, you can go back a stage until your child is ready and able to move forward again. Characteristic of helping children with learning difficulties, is that there will be times when you will need to put in a lot of effort for relatively small gains.

It is important not to allow any individual session to turn into a battle. You need to be firm and insistent but also try to have a good time. Give sensible (but not ecstatic) praise for progress, however small the step. Tell your child that you are pleased but also that this progress is only what you expected. Try to avoid criticism when your child starts to struggle; it is likely that there will be difficulties along the way. And when your child starts to move forward, your attitude should imply that you are sure that further progress will take place, following continued effort.

Sometimes, too much praise can make older children feel that they are being belittled. Some of the exercises are not so difficult and being praised for what is obviously quite easy, can be demoralising. Far more important than praise, is to refrain from criticism and resist the very natural tendency to show frustration or impatience. With older children, you can openly discuss and explain the purpose of any of the exercises, in particular those that they find hard or that make them tired. Show that you value their opinion.

Matters of Timing

Try to set by a certain time of day for the main session of training, preferably before your child becomes too tired, and, whenever possible, aim to keep to that same time. Do not make any of the sessions too heavy or too lengthy at first. As a general guide, start by doing the exercises for a few minutes every day and work up to around thirty to thirty five minutes, three or four times a week. The rate of the build up will depend on the speed of progress that your child can handle, but as a guide, expect the time spent to gradually increase over a period of around three months.

It can be important not to make each session too lengthy, so consider having a break and then starting again. An ideal arrangement, if it is practical, is for the session to last for around twenty minutes, with a break of half an hour and after that, to continue for another fifteen minutes.

By carrying out these exercises, you are directly addressing areas of weakness in the mental processes. This can be tiring, in the same way as if you were carrying out strengthening exercises for a physical weakness. If the pressure of doing an exercise gets to be too much, then break for a few minutes, encourage your child to have a drink and possibly a snack, and then recommence. Also, do not underestimate the effect on the trainer. Teaching is tiring and sometimes you will be working at quite a high degree of intensity with your child. You may be pleased to have a coffee break at the same time.

In many families, there is an older brother or sister, or perhaps a younger sibling, who will be much quicker with the answers than the child that you are trying to help. Whenever it is practical, try to arrange the session for a time when you can most easily prevent this intrusion and thus ensure that the child needing help will receive it without interference. Some of the exercises can be done as a family game but others require dedicated time and privacy.

Training The Teenager

Adolescent children usually need a somewhat different approach to that which is suitable for the younger child. Most of the time, younger children will do the exercises because they are fun and they enable them to have prime time with a parent. With older children, you may need to be much more direct and explain to them, from the outset, the purpose and the intent of what they are doing.

Sometimes, teenage children try very hard and the more they work at some exercises, the more extreme can be the tiredness that builds up. They are training their brains to make connections in a different way to anything that they have done before and are trying to bridge a gap that has developed over many years. Children are usually physically and mentally refreshed, simply by having a drink of water. It can be helpful to have a jug of water and a glass available from the start. You can liken the memory training process to physical training in a gymnasium. Building up physical strength and stamina also requires sustained exertion and the effort and the achievement are both part of the process.

Measuring Progress

There is often a great sense of elation, arising from small successes at the beginning. Children are encouraged, when they begin to see the light at the end of a very dark tunnel. In order to exploit this success, we recommend that you develop a recording process. The simple example that follows, shows how you might record progress for each of the various exercises. By noting the results in this way, both you and your child can see the pace of progress very clearly and you can identify the exercises in which they are improving and those that they are finding difficult. Recording and acknowledging the successes is a vital part of the process and the confidence this gives, will often lead to even greater success. We must remember that older children with learning difficulties may, previously, only have experienced failure. Therefore, do not start the overt monitoring process until there has been some success that can be identified, measured, and recorded.

The Progress Record

We suggest that you keep a book for recording the progress in each of the exercises that you undertake with your child. An easy way of doing this is to have a notebook with a separate page for each exercise. We suggest that you make a note *of each time there is a change* and you have made progress. In this way, you can view and measure progress over a period of time and you can look back and see the success you are achieving. You will also have a record of the stage that you have reached, when you come to carry out the exercise the next time. It is important to keep the recording process simple and to minimise the time it takes; otherwise such records are rarely maintained for long.

You will need to record the date and outcome of the activity. A simple and effective way of doing this is by use of the 'smiley'. Against each entry, you can draw a face, to record your assessment of how well your child managed the stage of the exercise that you reached. We suggest that you use the following conventions:

Smiley –success, possibly ready to move onto the next stage.
Straight–face –reasonable try, repeat next time to consolidate.
Glum –struggled, found it to be hard, try the same exercise next time or go back a stage.

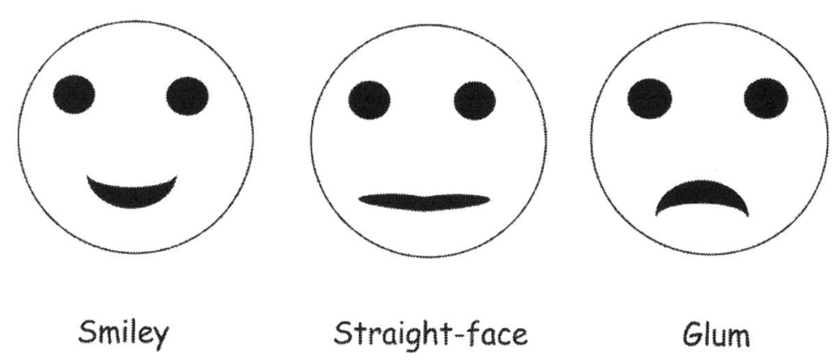

When you first commence the exercise, record the date and the stage that you reached. Most exercises start from a fairly low point, so the first few times that you carry out the exercise, you will probably append the smiley face. Following that, when your child is unable to complete a stage in the exercise, you record a glum face. (This is the point that the exercise starts to become remedial.) A second face can be used to record degrees of confidence, optimism or worry.

You do not need to make another entry, until there is a noticeable change or improvement. When that happens, you record the date and perhaps a straight-face for a change/some progress, or a smiley face when that particular stage of the exercise can be accomplished readily and it is time to move on.

A simple example is shown, for one of the dice exercises.

Exercise 10/1

Date	Stage Reached	Assessment
4 June	three dice in a line	☺
6 June	four dice in a line	☹ ☹
2 July	four dice in a line	☺

Expect To Succeed

Do not be discouraged by what may have transpired in the past with your child or by a history of frustration, in your contact with educationalists, psychiatrists or counsellors, who may have had little or no impact. Many children have come to the Turnabout Programme with a long history of failed interventions by others and have then turned things round and have been successful. By carrying out these training exercises with your child, you are following a well-trodden path and you will be enhancing the future prospects for your child's education and future.

Chapter Seventeen

Living in a Structured Environment

Many young people with a learning disability have difficulty in making the choices and decisions required for everyday life. Some become overly passive and do not react to events taking place around them; some display an excessive indifference and do not seem to care what happens. Others, particularly those diagnosed as 'hyperactive', have difficulty in staying within bounds; they are impulsive and they over-react to minor incidents.

These attitudes become ingrained and may well prevail, even when their learning capabilities are changing. And yet, within all of their social interactions, they are expected to be organised people. In the English primary school, together with the rest of the class, they are required to keep their desk or drawer tidy, to put their work in the right place and always have a pencil to hand. Similarly, within the secondary school, pupils are expected to manage homework deadlines and to have the appropriate book available at the right time, all of which requires planning and organisation. Many young people cannot live up to these basic expectations.

These organisational skills can be developed and encouraged within the home. It has been our experience that, in order to move forward effectively and to make the most of the Turnabout Programme, such children need to live within a structured home environment. If the way that they have interrelated with their home previously has been very free and easy, they are helped by changes that provide a more regular household routine. A home environment that restricts the choices that children are required to make and which simplifies and brings order into their daily routine, gives them the framework on which to build and manage their lives, when they are outside of the home. Children can be encouraged to have a calm approach and orderly thoughts in all they do, if the life they lead is reasonably planned and consistent.

The Turnabout concept of a structured home environment is, perhaps, different to what might be expected and it extends further than just the day-to-day routine of the child, important as that is. We believe that parents of children with serious learning difficulties, need to base the whole of their interaction with their child on improving the way the child is able to input and retrieve information. We then have the ideal situation, where all aspects of life in the home, support and reinforce the changes taking place through the Turnabout exercises.

Set out in this chapter, we provide suggestions and recommendations, showing how you can greatly help your children, by focussing very directly on the way that you deal with them in day-to-day matters. This includes planning and controlling the time in front of the television, setting out to talk to your children in a way that will assist them to marshal their thoughts and to communicate better, formalising your approach to the way they listen to stories, and guiding and influencing the quantity and nature of their physical activity.

Within the home, it is important that events should be planned ahead and should not just 'happen'. Changes to the home environment may need to encompass all of the main domestic arrangements, such as maintaining a set time for eating and for sleeping, and also planning and scheduling after school activities and other social activities. As part of implementing this approach, it is usually helpful to agree a schedule for the week ahead, so that, together with your child, you can discuss and decide what is going to happen on each day of the week that follows.

If you intend to set out a more formalised approach and re-plan the daily routine of your child, the strategy should be introduced gradually. Nevertheless, you must state very clearly what is important for you in the way that you want the house to operate and what is not. It is necessary for all of the members of the family to be party to the agreement. A family cannot easily set more lenient or stricter standards for the dyslexic or ADHD child, than for the other children.

Very often, children with learning problems are difficult to deal with and parents can be tempted to give-in, to avoid yet another confrontation. Consistently backing down to your child is a losing strategy. A disciplined and ordered lifestyle for children is a vital and essential base for rebuilding their self-confidence and helping them to manage in the world outside of their home. You do not need to accept and to live with self-indulgence from the younger child or the self-destructive outbursts of the adolescent child.

For teenagers who have been used to a fairly free and easy life, creating a more structured environment, with rules, can represent quite a change to their whole lifestyle. There will no doubt be disagreements and no child will ever want any additional constraints. But the normal psychology of all children, including those that have difficulties, is that they want to be valued by their family and they would really like to be successful and regain their self-esteem. Based on compromises on each side, it is usually possible for an agreed (even if tentative) routine to be established, which will entail a greater degree of structure being brought back into the household.

Each and every family situation is different, and no set of rules will be applicable in every case. Making changes to a child's lifestyle is never easy and it becomes more problematic, the older your child is when you start. We make no apology for recommending a formalised family environment, but, in the end, it is for you the parents, to decide for yourselves, what is appropriate and what is achievable, in your own circumstances.

Managing Television Time

Television is often a focal point in the life of the younger child. We strongly recommend that television time needs to be controlled and managed. For most primary age children, an hour a day of television is sufficient and will leave time for doing something that requires more active involvement. Although it can be very convenient to allow children to settle down in front of the television armed with the remote control device, a better approach is to hold on to the remote control yourself, and try to guide television watching to the more intelligent and educational programs, or to proper plays and stories. Even better, is to plan the television programmes at the start of the week, so that television becomes an integral part of the structured family life.

Our own experience, which is supported by recent studies in the United States, has shown very clearly that an excess of television can be greatly detrimental for the young child. Overexposure to television can directly contribute to learning difficulties. We have seen that children, who have spent many consecutive hours watching television, become passive and uninvolved in their whole outlook. Too much television can hold back mental development, diminish the concentration span and inhibit personal development. The Turnabout exercises will not be fully effective, if the increased powers of concentration that they engender are undermined by long passive periods in front of the flashing screen of a television. A change to the pattern of watching television can be an important part of the turnabout for many children.

Plan to watch a televised film, DVD or video, together with your children, and at the end of it, try to encourage them to think about it and to talk about it. Ask them to discuss the characters in the film and whether or not they were realistic and believable. By discussing the twists and turns of the plot, a child begins to develop the ability to think about the story and then be able to tell it back, in the sequence it happened. Without any major change to routine, this will help to develop an improved ability to retain information and to recall it.

Listening To Stories

Activities that involve listening to spoken language are to be encouraged. Children of all ages enjoy listening to a story on tape or CD. There is a wonderful range of 'talking books' available, for you to choose something suitable for your own child to listen to. After the story is finished, it is worth spending a few minutes discussing the story and the characters, in the same way as we have suggested for reviewing films on television.

Listening to a story and at the same time, attempting to read the words of the book, can be a valuable experience for children. This task is by no means as easy as it might appear. Some dyslexic children will find it difficult at first, as they are attempting to use two senses at the same time. It may be confusing for them to follow the story in a book, while they are listening to it. But it does not matter if a child cannot read the words very well. It should be a pleasurable experience and not a test of ability or progress. Children should be encouraged to follow in the book, as best as they can.

For the younger child, you can play a well-liked story many times over and encourage your child to learn the words by heart. Stories repeated over and over again, bring a familiarity that helps children to process and understand information more readily. The act of learning by heart, can be part of the training in storing and retrieving language and can help children who have difficulty listening to and then absorbing, information within the classroom.

You can go further and this will bring additional benefits. Following some books, ask your child to set out the main points of the narrative. This can be done by writing a simple list; one word or phrase representing each feature or action will be sufficient, or by drawing pictures of the story or by talking about it; the most appropriate method will depend on the age and ability of the child. Writing a list of key words or phrases can also be done with televised films. This process of summarising the main points will help a child to be able to listen and learn in the classroom.

Structured Conversations

As parents, you can greatly assist the retraining process by maintaining (or perhaps re-establishing) a regular dialogue with your child, but in such a way as to enhance and complement the training programme. We have discussed many times, that an important aspect of the Turnabout exercises is to help children to be able to select the information that is more important or relevant and to disregard other extraneous detail. You can support this process by the way that you talk to your children, being careful to guide the discussion towards a structured conversation.

An ideal opportunity can be when you ask about what has happened during the day at school (or anywhere else). If the explanation tends to ramble on around the topic, as is quite common, then, at that point, call a halt to the conversation and encourage your child to start again and be much more direct. Children should be asked to describe the events of their day *in the sequence that they happened* and to be careful and concise with their explanation. The changeover from rambling to a logical sequence will be a gradual one. It is best not to impose this change too forcefully or in a derogatory way but something like "I am only the parent and do not really understand", seems to work most of the time.

Whenever you can, try to guide your child towards this style of conversation, building a logical sequence into explanations and descriptions of events. Discussions of this type will help to develop a better ability to organise and structure information within the memory. It will also give your child practice in being able to sequence into a logical pattern and select from a mass of detail. For many children, this will be directly contrary to the way they have been used to thinking and communicating.

Discussions of this nature develop a child's capability to explain themselves better, in all circumstances. The use of language in a controlled way is fundamental to being able to communicate thoughts correctly, promptly and concisely. Children who are able to express themselves clearly and accurately, develop better social skills and greater self-control than others, and are more easily able to mix in a wide variety of environments. There is a direct causal relationship between the ability to communicate and the ability to absorb new information, so it is of great potential benefit to guide your child towards clearer and more succinct communication.

The Approach to Physical Exercise

Many children with dyslexia do not have good physical co-ordination, balance or ball skills. All exercise is worthwhile, but try to guide your child to take up activities that develop these particular attributes. Activities that require co-ordinated movements between the left and right sides of the body can have particular benefit for the dyslexic child. Many ball sports will be helpful in this respect, but some children with poor co-ordination will do their best to avoid sport or other competitive physical activity, to prevent embarrassment. For children who do not like contact or competitive sport, aerobics to music is strenuous and excellent for improving physical co-ordination.

It has been well publicised that many children receive an inadequate amount of physical exercise and that obesity is a growing concern. Increased obesity is generally accompanied by diminished self-esteem, and for this reason alone, even if for no other, it should be discouraged. While carrying out the Turnabout process of personal and mental development, it is important not to neglect the physical aspect. If children do not undertake sport or dance or are not physically active in some other way, try to persuade and encourage them that this would be both beneficial and enjoyable. Practise with the martial arts can also be helpful for those young people that take to it. Judo is good for physical and mental co-ordination, as is Karate. Practising Judo can bring about a much greater sense of spatial awareness. The formalised sets of movements (Katas) within Karate are likely to be difficult at first for dyslexic people, due to the need to remember the sequence of actions, but they are an effective means of memory training.

Physical exercise supports the learning process. If your child is not physically active, try to institute a period of around five minutes of aerobics, perhaps in conjunction with a video, before each session of Turnabout exercises.

What The Parents Say

"As a mother of a thirteen year old child, who could not keep up with the other children in her class, who could not express herself verbally and who could not read properly, I was helpless and didn't know how to help her.

The one thing that I remember from my first meeting with Carol is her explanation of dyslexia. She explained that dyslexia could be compared to road works along the road, which causes traffic to back up. Carol explained that in Tina's case, she has a word block and that we have to find ways to bypass the problem.

Carol's method turned the whole situation around. Today, three years later, Tina is a successful student. She reads fluently, manages long texts in school, tires less and her results in most of her studies are very good. Tina is highly motivated and has positive self-esteem. She knows that she has to work hard, but feels very proud that she has learnt how to cope with her problem, turn the situation around and succeed.

Words cannot express my thanks".

"Angie is now in her final year at school. She was on the programme for only two years and now no longer needs extra help.

Thank you for everything. We just cannot believe how well adjusted Angie has become. She is managing very well. I have no words to thank you for what you have given us by helping her. She is doing so well - way beyond our expectations! Thank you."

Chapter Eighteen

Rebuilding Self-Esteem

We have discussed previously, how low self-esteem can present a barrier to learning. This applies to children of all ages but is most particularly the case with teenagers, in whom a lack of self-confidence can become very strongly entrenched. This chapter of the book advises parents on the problematic but most important task, of boosting the confidence of their teenage children, so that whatever their children attempt to do, they do to the best of their ability.

Coping with Failure

Nobody really wants to fail, but dyslexic people may well have experienced failure many times. For such people, a vital part of attempting to move forward is not to spend too much time looking back or worrying about previous lack of success. To be able to do this is not as straightforward as it might appear. Within the competitive western society, our upbringing does not always give us the tools to cope with failure, either in ourselves or in our children. When children are experiencing difficulties at school, both child and parent can react emotionally. We must reflect and understand that, for all of us, life is not one continuous flow of success. Young people and their parents must be able to accept and deal with setbacks, as a precursor to re-building self-esteem.

This chapter is concerned with helping your teenage children to be realistic and to see their situation in a new light. We recommend a very positive approach. We should encourage young people to look forward in an optimistic way. The prevailing attitude needs to be along the lines of the following:

"OK, things have not gone well. We know that nothing has come easily for you at school. Now, at last, you have got a good chance. By your own efforts using these Turnabout exercises, you have the opportunity of success. Now it is time to start to look at life in a different way."

First of all, we need to assess for ourselves and discuss with our children, some very basic issues surrounding lack of success. By what scale are we measuring, when we think that we have failed or that our child has failed? What we sometimes perceive as failure is an unrealistic comparison with others, who may seem to be doing better. It is important to emphasise that failure is not a permanent state and it is not a disaster! We all fail at something in our lives sooner or later. An apparent failure is largely a matter of how we perceive ourselves. The athlete who achieves a 'personal best', but comes last in the race, has not failed. The child who is making progress in school is not failing, irrespective of the attainment of others. The barrier that children must overcome is the mindset of "I can't do it because I have tried before and I failed then, so, if I try again, I am bound to fail".

We need to attempt to restore and rebuild self-belief, so that perceptions of inadequacy will no longer be an obstruction to moving forward. In order to begin to bring this about, we need to encourage young people to take a mature approach and to begin to look at and assess themselves objectively.

Towards a Positive Self-image

As soon as young people have begun to recognise and accept that a previous lack of success need not be permanent state, then they can redefine their whole approach to life, in a far more positive way.

They can then commence the important task of building up a strong self-image. The Turnabout methodology separates the process of building self-esteem into four overlapping stages. The main intent is for young people to begin to understand themselves and to feel good about themselves.

Stage 1. Beginning Self-Assessment

As a first step towards an improved self-image, we recommend that young people, with the help and support of their parents, undertake a process of **self-assessment**. This should to take place in a controlled and structured way. We have provided a guide that will enable your teenage children, with your help, to assess where they stand within any aspect of their lives. View and consider the 'Ladder of Attainment' that follows.

The Ladder of Attainment

⇧ ***Success***
⇧ ***Achievement***
⇧ ***Improvement***
⇧ ***Motivation***
⇧ ***Involvement***
⇧ ***Assessment***
⇧ ***Apparent Failure***
⇧ ***Despair***
⇧ ***Alienation***

Probably the first thing that we should note from this table is that it presents an approach to how we view 'failure', that is different to the perceptions of many people. We need to begin to look at what has seemed to be failure, as just a step on the ladder, a point on a scale from which we can go up or down. We can see from the ladder of attainment that *apparent failure* is not the lowest rung on the ladder and *it is not a permanent state.* It should be viewed as a position within the table and it must be seen as a *temporary state.*

We should recognise that there is much worse that can happen to any individual than lack of success. Lapsing into *despair,* the lower rung on the ladder is worse than just having failed at something. Parental influence can play a crucial role, by preventing a child who has a perception of failure, from slipping down into pessimism and despair.

If feelings of despair continue for too long, this can bring about descent to the lowest point on the scale, which we define as '*alienation*'. Alienation is the state of '*I don't really care any more*' and it can instil within people, coldness and remoteness in their personality, that in some cases can cause them to step away and to drop out from society.

You must encourage your child to look forward in a positive way. Progress is usually made only in small steps. The first move upwards on the ladder from apparent failure is to *assessment.* Assessment is the state where your child will be able to look at life a little more clearly and assess or re-assess:

"What has happened to me?"

"Where am I in my school life?"

"Where am I in my personal life?"

For children who have had problems in school, the process of assessment may bring about the realisation that, by their own standards, they might have made some good improvement, even if others around them seem to be finding life somewhat easier.

From assessment, the next step up the ladder is *involvement.* For the person who is still finding things difficult, involvement can be just making a small start, setting some modest goals but becoming a 'player in the game' or perhaps, just rejoining the game. For some, commencing the Turnabout Programme will itself be a sign of involvement. The important thing is making a start; making the effort however small and becoming involved.

This first move, making a small start and beginning to be involved, will usually lead to greater commitment. The gradual improvement in self-confidence that this will instil, leads naturally to moving up onto the next rung of the ladder, which is *motivation.* Motivation is the opposite of alienation; it is a desire or a willingness to show to others or to prove to yourself, that you can do something. Children who have suffered a number of setbacks in their lives may take some time to reach this stage, but when they get there, it can be the springboard for more rapid advance.

When a person has become motivated to succeed, then it is usually not too long before this motivation begins to take effect. It can soon become apparent that there has been some noticeable *improvement,* which is the next step up the ladder. The definition of improvement is that there are results that can be seen and measured.

A measurable improvement, however small, is important. This improvement will allow the individual to make a further step upwards, to a state in which something worthwhile and tangible has been accomplished; something that can be judged as an *achievement.*

Having strived to achieve something worthwhile, further effort will gradually lead to the top point in the table, which is *success.* Success can be many different things for different people. For the severely dyslexic person, success can be the act of taking the very first steps in learning, perhaps by being able to read a book or even a page, without assistance. For the person who has been troubled by ADHD, success may perhaps be defined as 'sitting through the lesson and being just like everyone else'.

We can see from the ladder of attainment, that it is vitally important that young people do not view a time of *apparent failure* as a permanent state. Even if they have yet to be able to accomplish anything significant in their lives, that is a situation that only relates to today. In time, movement up the ladder can be made by anyone.

Some teenagers can relate to a sporting analogy. For people who have not succeeded at sport, a few months in the gymnasium with the weights and some intensive work on the running track, might well start a move up the sporting attainment table. Similarly, those who have had difficulty with their schooling should re-assess themselves, after carrying out the Turnabout exercises for some time. Whatever has happened in the past must be regarded just as one rung on the ladder of attainment. Young people must believe that they have it in them to progress, step by step, to the top of the ladder.

Stage 2. Encouraging Self-Awareness

The second part of building towards enhanced self-esteem is to bring about greater **self-awareness.** This is about young people understanding that they are worthwhile in their own right, believing in themselves and not making comparisons with other people. (Parents also need to avoid making judgements about their children that compare them with others.)

This step in the development of a positive self-image involves acceptance of, '*Who I am and where I am, in my home and in my school life*'. It is the pivotal point in building a positive self-image. If children have aspects of dyslexia or are struggling with attention deficit problems, they must come to terms with accepting themselves as they are, with both their strengths and their areas for improvement.

There are positive and negative aspects of self-awareness. A way to encourage the positive aspects is for parents to talk with their children, with the very direct intention of boosting their sense of well-being. Try to encourage young people to find ways of feeling good about themselves. Emphasise their strengths, try to minimise any jocular disparagement by brothers or sisters, avoid comparisons with others. It can sometimes be helpful to discuss family history and to talk about interesting or worthy members of the family, looking as far back in time as you can go, so that your children can develop a sense of belonging and identity.

Many people have been encouraged and inspired by the thought that they are descended from someone who was brave or clever or upright, and that they have inherited some of these genes and characteristics. Sometimes, we are motivated by knowledge of great grandparents, who overcame various difficulties in their lives. Many British citizens are descended from immigrants, and stories of how these people managed to travel, adapt and to thrive, can inspire young teenagers to confront their own problems with just a little more determination. However you bring it about, it is necessary that you persuade and support your child in this first important move to greater self-awareness.

But, equally important for young people, is for them to be aware of and to accept, all aspects of their personality. They must recognise and understand their quirks of character, their idiosyncrasies, their strengths and particularly their weaknesses. They must see these for what they are and be willing to move forward.

"I know that I have a bad temper. I accept the fact and will try to do something about it."

"I know I have a trigger point. I get embarrassed when I can't do something and I shout at people; my teachers, my parents and even my friends."

"I now know that I have a visual learning problem. I'm not very pleased, but I will work on it and try to improve."

This realism, this self-awareness, is an essential pre-requisite for both step three and step four of the process of building towards a positive self-image. Step three is about greater self-control; people must accept that this is necessary and they need to be aware of the areas of their life in which self-control needs to be applied. Step four is the process of self-regulation. To give effect to this, young people need to know themselves, so that they can begin to manage and take control of their lives. Self-awareness, self-control and self-regulation are the building blocks of greater self-esteem in the young person.

Stage 3. Building Self Control

The third stage in the process of regaining self-esteem is the establishment of **self-control**. This is basically about restraint; not being impulsive or throwing tantrums or losing control over minor matters. Young people have to start to accept that the time has come to stop blaming others,

for things not working out. There can no longer be self-justification by blaming teachers, or the school, or parents or anyone else. Your teenage children have to be encouraged to take responsibility for themselves. This is often the hardest part of the process. It is characteristic of adolescents, that they have a tendency to blame other people, or the institutions, or bad luck, or an unhelpful world, for each and every one of their problems. You may need to persuade your children to make the change, away from thinking about who to blame, towards acceptance of the situation. "*I accept that I have not done too well and I am beginning to know what I need to do, so that I can start making a change*".
This process of taking control can sometimes be boosted by noticeable progress with the Turnabout exercises and the consequent improvements in memory and the ability to learn.

Stage 4. Self Regulation

The fourth step towards a positive self-image is **self-regulation**. This is the state of being able to understand yourself and to regulate yourself throughout your daily life. A practical example of self-regulation might be "*I know that I can learn better in the morning, so I will do my homework on Sunday morning and then do other things in the afternoon, rather than leave everything until the last possible moment*". Self-regulation sees teenagers begin to look ahead and plan and control what they are doing. The role of taking responsibility is moving away from the parents to the child and as parents, you need to do all that you can to encourage this.

When you see an element of self-regulation being adopted by your teenage child, you will know that you are starting to reach your target. This is the time that you can see young people begin to take control of their schoolwork and of other major aspects of their lives. They have reached a state of understanding themselves and of feeling comfortable with themselves. The better we are able to understand ourselves, the easier it is to control our feelings and to predict ahead how we need to behave in pressured situations. In very many cases, when once disruptive teenagers have reached the point of being able to regulate themselves, it has brought great relief to the whole family. The stresses and frustrations of seeming to fail, may previously have induced tiredness and lethargy. The process that we have set out can itself be energising.

Self-regulation is the aim, and usually, it is only when this state is reached, that your child's self-esteem will begin to settle at the level that you are seeking. A state of self-regulation will come about when the underlying foundations are in place. In order to bring about this mature state, all of the matters discussed in this chapter will need to have been addressed. (The topic of self-regulation is taken a little further in the following chapter.)

Summary

Improving your teenage child's self esteem is a vital part of the Turnabout Programme, almost as important as the exercises for enhancing a child's mental capabilities. The main things that you can do to help to bring this about are summarised below, in a logical sequence of events.

Apparent Failure to Success – The Tools for Life

- Eliminate or minimise external negative influences.
- Understand that failure is temporary
- Accept that the Ladder of Attainment is a true representation of life.
- Accept that apparent failure is just a point on the scale
- Undergo a process of self-assessment
- Develop greater self-awareness - strengths and weaknesses.
- Develop greater self –control
- Carry out the process of self-regulation
- Progress up the ladder of attainment - from apparent failure to success

Chapter Nineteen

Integrating into School Life

This chapter is intended primarily for the benefit of teenagers; young people who have worked through the Turnabout programme and whose reading and writing have now improved sufficiently, so that they can become part of the regular school learning process.

Throughout the whole of their school career, these young people may well have been sitting quite passively through the lessons, with only minimal understanding and very limited participation. But now, there has been a change in their capabilities. As a direct result of the Turnabout exercises and not least, of their own determination, they have the possibility of success. But our experience has been that these young people can find it difficult to start to adapt themselves to a full school life. They may now be able to read and write sufficiently well to participate in the lessons; they may be able to understand and react to the teacher's instructions; but sometimes they do not really comprehend the nature of the academic process, nor are they able to manage themselves within it. This chapter sets out to provide them with the help and guidance they need to make the most of their emerging abilities and begin to succeed. We have broken down the process of managing life in a secondary school environment into separate discrete steps – *the ten-point plan.*

At this point, the final chapter of the book, we think it is appropriate to address the comments and the advice, directly to the young people themselves. Continuing the theme of self-regulation discussed in the previous chapter, this is a part of their life that they must come to terms with themselves and take responsibility for. Of course we would expect you, the parents, to guide and help but, in the end, teenagers need to manage these matters for themselves. We need commitment as a forerunner to success.

Here then, for the teenager, is **your ten-point plan.**

You may chose to take it all on ..... or you may just want to use some of the advice.

You may look at it as a way of helping to bring structure to your life ..... or you may chose just to use it as a study guide, to give you the 'know how' that others seem to have acquired.

However you wish to approach it, these are ten steps in the process of 'self-regulation', of managing your own rate of progress; leading to control of your life and to as much success as you are able and determined to achieve.

Ten Steps In The Process of Self-regulation.

1. Where are you starting from?

At the start, you will find that it will help you to move forward, if you can make a frank assessment of yourself - where you now stand in the process of commencing your education proper and of managing your life. This is a time to be realistic and honest with yourself; to set out your strengths and also your weaknesses. It is not easy to be really frank and honest about yourself but it will be worth the effort.

Look at and consider such matters as:

* What can you do now that you could not do before your Turnabout training?
* What are the most important things that you still cannot do?

Try to produce a short list of things that have improved a great deal following your Turnabout training and others that have improved less or hardly at all. Be very honest with yourself and write it all down or key it into the computer, so that you can come back to it later and see how you are progressing. (You may ask for help from your parents to get you started.)

Such a self-assessment statement might be something like: -

JOHN SMITH - age 15
Strengths
Still have an attention problem
Getting much better
Try hard.
Good at Science
Better at Maths than I was.
Read a lot of magazines - not many books.
Weaknesses
Find it hard to sit still
Cannot concentrate for the whole lesson.
Not good at writing things down.
Sometimes don't finish what I start.
Friends.
Only five friends at school.
Not sure what to say to girls.
Quiet in a large group.
Family
Don't get on with Dad. We argue about school.
Younger brothers are a pain -little sister is nice.
Get on well with grandma who lives in Scotland.

By setting things down in this way, you start to see, not only the sort of person you are now but also who you want to be. For example, the list might show how you would like to interact with family and friends and what level of short-term success you might sensibly be capable of aiming for.

Start off by honestly assessing yourself as a person and also as a student.

2. How do you function best?

Although it doesn't always show, most of us would really like to do well. In this competitive world, it is very important that you give yourself the very best chance of succeeding. There is no escape from the four-letter word - **work!** But you can and should try to arrange to work at the time and place and in the manner that suits you best. You will need to assess yourself honestly and think how you can make the most of your own nature; how you can make use of your strengths and in particular, how you can compensate for your weaknesses. Think about such things as:

* **When do you work best, in the morning or the evening?** Some of us are at our best early in the day and others don't really come to life until later.
* **Do you learn better with music playing loudly**, or is it really self-indulgence and a distraction?
* **Can you take phone calls while you are trying to do schoolwork** or do they disturb and distract you and should you really switch off your mobile phone?
* **Can you study with other people around?** Some people need the privacy and quiet of their own room. How does it work for you?
* **How long can you concentrate for at a time?** Some people can keep going for a couple of hours, while others need to take a short break every twenty minutes or so.

You will want to be a success at school and in your life, so try to plan and organise your time so that you are giving yourself the best possible chance.

3. Understanding yourself.

Step three is the sometimes complex process of understanding yourself emotionally as a person; knowing you own moods, knowing your high and your low points; trying to make the most of your own personality. For example there are many people who are not at their best when they are tired or hungry and a self analysis for a person in this category might be: -

"Sometimes I get tired, then I feel irritable, I don't handle things well and what starts out as a discussion can turn into a confrontation. Therefore, I will try to deal with people and with difficult situations only in the morning. And when we are all hungry, my parents and I are all a bit snappy, so I will try to make sure that we discuss awkward matters after a meal, when everyone is a little more relaxed."

As mentioned previously, some of us are morning people and some come to life in the evenings. By understanding yourself as a person and by making the best of your own personal characteristics, you will help your relationships with your school, your family, and your friends.

Be aware of yourself and try to deal with awkward situations, serious discussions, occasional confrontations, when you are best able to handle the situation.

4. What do I have to do?

This may sound like a very simple and obvious question but surprisingly, many young people in secondary school and even some college students, have never considered the basic aspects of how to study. For everything that you are asked to do, for every task that you are given, you should consider whether or not you are clear: -

* **What do I really have to do?**
* **When do I have to do it by?**

And, not least

* **How will I know when I have done it?**

Knowing what you need to do to function properly in the classroom is an important aspect of self-regulation, of managing your own life. For some subjects, such as mathematics, this will usually be quite obvious. But, for other subjects, it may not be at all clear what has to be done. For example, it may not be obvious - how many pages need to be written, which words of a foreign language must you know and which words can you look up when you need them, or what standard of writing, spelling and English grammar is expected. Teachers and lecturers often assume that students know these things but many students are more than a little uncertain.

You will probably need to ask your teachers, you may have to discuss this with your friends, but do not start any work until you are fairly confident that you can answer the three questions:

What do I need to do? - By when? - How will I know when it is done?

5 What do I know? What don't I know?

Although this is similar to the previous point, understanding what you need to do is not the same as understanding what you need to *know* and *learn*. Each of the subjects that you study has its own body of knowledge. You need to realise where you stand in acquiring a sufficient level of knowledge. This is also not always straightforward, but it can be very helpful to think about each subject in a structured and analytical way. Try to assess your work for all subjects or major part of the subject, under the categories below.

* ***What do I actually know?***
* ***What don't I know?*** Try to recognise when you don't know something specific.
* ***What do I need to know*** - in order to answer a question, to pass a test, to complete a project, to cope with an examination, or even for your own interest and satisfaction?

This way of looking at your work is known as 'comprehension monitoring'; which is a process of changing your approach from saying that "I can't cope", or "I don't know," or "I can't do maths", to saying, "I can do this and go that far, but when I get to something else, I need to ask".

When you start, it may not be easy to think about your schoolwork in this way. If you have difficulty with this process then try to enlist a school friend or teacher to help you, or a parent or someone else suitable. Other children can often be very helpful and supportive and sometimes it is surprising to find out how many people welcome the opportunity to help someone else.

Analyse what you know and don't know, for every subject that you are studying.

6 Never Be Ashamed Or Unwilling To Ask For Help.

This is probably the most important aspect of the ten-point plan. It is not easy. You may find asking for help to be embarrassing and indeed, many people find it difficult throughout their lives. But it is very important. Use your list of what you need to know more about and ask for help with these specific topics. Ask the teachers; they are usually pleased and fulfilled when someone has asked for their help. You may also find that your teachers will continue to give you guidance and support. If they do, then accept whatever comes your way and take no notice of any banter from your schoolmates. The help is for your benefit and nobody else's. If your teacher is not approachable or helpful, then ask a friend or ask someone in your family, ask in the library for a suitable book, and keep on asking, until you start to get some answers and you are sure that you are getting all the help that you need.

Persist! Don't feel uncomfortable, just because you fear that your questions might be very basic and obvious and you think you might feel foolish when you are given the answer. Once you start asking for help, it usually becomes easier each time. If you get a rebuff or a belittling answer, don't let it unsettle you.

Keep on asking!

7 Checklist the Main Points.

When you have covered a specific topic in a lesson at school, you should attempt, in your own time, to make a list of the most important points. A good way of doing this is to start with an introduction that summarises what the topic is about, and then follow that with a list of all of the main facts that you know on the subject. The list does not have to be in a logical sequence. Making a checklist is in line with other aspects of the Turnabout training; being able to select the significant features and discard those of lesser importance. In fact, the act of making out the checklist will help you to understand and to remember the topic as a whole.

Making a list and picking out the important points, can be confusing at first, particularly for those who have previously had difficulties with their schoolwork. It is not always clear and straightforward what are the most important points to learn about any subject. But identifying and selecting the key points is the basis of any form of study. It is a skill, which has to be acquired, by repetition and by the process of trying it out and improving with practice. Here again, do not worry about asking for assistance from your parents or from anyone else. You will find that there will be a gradual but definite improvement in your abilities to write these checklists and eventually you will be able to manage it without anyone else's help.

Making a checklist will help you to understand and remember.

8 Beginning to Take Control

This action and the two actions that follow are a continuation of the process of self-regulation, described in the previous chapter. Self-regulation is the process of understanding yourself better and taking control of your own life.

This action, the beginning of taking control of your own learning, should take place after you have spent some months reaping the benefit of the improvements brought about by the Turnabout exercises. You need to step back and review all of the subjects you are studying or projects that you are working on, but in a formalised and mature way. Think about each aspect of your schoolwork and as you do, you will find that you are beginning to take control.

For each subject that you study, you should review these matters and set out your own checklist:

* ***What is demanded of me? What do I need to do?***
* ***Can I do what is demanded?***
* ***Can I set some goals for myself? Particularly timescales.***
* ***How much do I know?***
* ***In what categories do I not know enough (or anything)?***
* ***What can I do about my weaknesses?***
* ***What can I achieve? By when?***
* ***How will I get there? How do I plan my time?***
* ***How am I going to seek help?***
* ***Who is available to ask for help?***

Sometimes it is difficult not to be discouraged by the scope of a subject. The history of a period or an aspect of science may seem to contain an overwhelmingly large body of knowledge. But for each subject, you will find that it can be broken down into - the most significant *facts that you need to know*, the most important *aspects that you need to understand* and the essential *skills that you must acquire*. Each element that you need to be familiar with can be separated out from the other detail, that might well be interesting but is not essential. You will almost certainly find that the effect of the memory training has been to help you to pick up far more knowledge than you realise at first.

You will reach the stage where you are able to start taking control. You should do it!

9. Evaluate Yourself Realistically

As a further aspect of taking control, it is a good idea to put yourself through a short self-evaluation. You can then repeat it every few months, on a regular basis. People are quite different in the way that they evaluate themselves. You can probably recognise, from amongst your friends, that some people have unrealistic expectations of themselves. They believe the task to be done is easy and are then amazed to find that they have failed. The other extreme is those people who come to see certain types of work or certain subjects as particularly formidable, (often it is mathematics). This fear of the subject can form a barrier that makes it difficult, even to make a start. Neither extreme is usually the true situation. It is important that you take a realistic look at each task that is ahead of you and assess your own ability to handle it.

You can attempt to evaluate yourself after a classroom session or a completed homework or a finished project. Assess how well you have done and accept the fact that it may well not have been a total success. This is not a tragedy, nor is it something that will necessarily be repeated in the long run. You need to make a start by reviewing each major piece of work: assess what you have done and how you might have done it better.

Evaluate yourself! This is part of making progress and of improving yourself as a student and as a person.

10. Continuous Review.

The process of personal evaluation, is something that many participants in the Turnabout Programme have been able to carry through from school to college, then to their work and indeed, into many aspects of their lives. You should aim to reach the point, where you regularly review and assess what you have done, and are realistically considering how you might do a little better next time, Be mature enough not to be motivated or discouraged by the praise or criticism from others (that you have probably grown up with). You are no longer part of that world. In its place, you need to set up a process of regular and continuous *self-review* (perhaps together with support from your family).

This review needs to look at all aspects of your life, in particular your academic life, but also include your family life, your social life and your personal conduct. Assess yourself in an honest and realistic way and once again set out a checklist:

* ***Where do I stand right now?***
* ***What have I done so far?***
* ***What have I still got to do?***
* ***What are my short term plans?***
* ***What are my medium term objectives?***
* ***Am I now ready to set out my long-term objectives?***
* ***If so, where am I heading?***
* ***Am I now ready to make a big push to be what I want to be?***
* ***And if not now, when?***

You can start to plan all aspects of your life. At first, try to do this for a period no longer than three months. Within this timeframe, set out your plans and targets but make sure that they are realistic and achievable. It can take some time to move away from a position where you were uncertain of the future, to realise that you are now able to think about long-term objectives. When you are ready, you can move on to planning for the medium and longer term and setting down in a more detailed way, where and what you would like to be and how you might achieve this.

You are now starting to take control of your life.

ISBN 141202955-4

9 781412 029551

Made in the USA
Lexington, KY
07 July 2013